As Sparks Fly Upward
Mom's Story

**The memories of
Crystal Hay**

To Tristyn
With love.
Faith Fisher
Kelowna BC
May 5, 2024

**Compiled and edited
and with additional information by
Faith Fisher**

Mill Lake Books

Published by Mill Lake Books
Chilliwack, BC
Canada
jamescoggins.wordpress.com/mill-lake-books

Cover photo copyright © iStockphoto.com. Used with permission.

ISBN: 978-1-998787-08-1

Table of Contents

In memory of
John Douglas Hay
1947–2019

PART ONE

FAMILY BACKGROUND

Introduction

Mom passed away in 2004, at age eighty-eight, after a sudden and brief illness.

At the request of my brother Frank, Mom had visited his home in Langley, British Columbia, in August 1998, to record some of the events of her life and the life of our family. Mom, then aged eight-two, was seated at a table on which were placed a box of photographs and a cassette recorder. The photos were there to stimulate memories and help Mom reflect on her life, and the story was recorded in an interview style. The cassette tapes were converted to compact discs (CDs) in 2014, and Frank distributed copies to his siblings.

In the spring of 2017, having previously retired and moved from Winnipeg, Manitoba, to Abbotsford, British Columbia, I took the time to upload the CDs to computer files. In May of that year, I and one other willing individual transcribed the recordings.

The idea of publishing Mom's story in book form was tossed about in my mind off and on until the pandemic year of 2021. I decided then that it was "now or never." Over the course of several months, Mom's reflections, now recorded and transcribed, were put into sequential order, titles were given to segments of her story, and research was done to corroborate times, dates, names, places and events.

Effort has been made to maintain Mom's "voice." However, in order to provide some background, to place segments in context and to supply pertinent information or clarity, some segments were modified. Footnotes have also been used so as not to interrupt the flow of the story.

Why Publish a Book?

After a review of a few segments of the manuscript, a reader asked me why I would want the story told, as it reveals some "unflattering details" about my family.

I thought I had answered that question for myself in the early months of writing and researching. I'm not sure now what that answer was. However, having pretty much completed the story, mulling that question over in my mind since and thinking deeply about it, here is why:

First, because my mother told it. She wanted Frank and her other children to see more clearly what our growing up years were like and why. I don't think there was any attempt on her part to hide or excuse what happened. She just wanted to help us understand it.

Following Mother's death in March 2004, we five siblings agreed to meet on the first weekend of June to begin to talk together, to try to gain some perspective on why we seemed to be what could be termed a "dysfunctional" family and to understand why we were unable to relate well with each other. We all knew our upbringing had a lot to do with it. That June weekend would be the first of five annual "sibling weekends." All of us were married and busy raising our own families. Our gained wisdom and experience at this point in life would help us in our understanding of the past.

There are fifteen years between the oldest and the youngest of our family. A five-year-old will have a different perspective than a nineteen-year-old when viewing the same thing. Each of us had a different perspective. I am the only female, which added a different dimension (I was known as "the favourite sister"). Our different personalities also contributed to our view of our lived experience. Talking about our life together gave us a window into each other's life experience that we had not previously known but could now begin to understand.

Second, Both Frank and I felt the need to pass the story on. For us, and I think the other siblings, there always seemed to have been some "mystery," some family secrets that had now been mostly revealed through Mom's telling of her story. It may be that our children and grandchildren will also become curious at some point in their lives and have a desire to know.

Third, I increasingly felt compelled to take on the project of putting Mom's story into print. It was even more than just feeling that I had no choice. It was more that I was being pulled into it and simply was not able to refuse.

Prior to delving into this story, throughout my life, I had always felt that I lived "on the fringe"—as if I was allowed to participate but was never fully accepted in the communities in which I lived from childhood to adulthood. I had not understood what others around me knew. It all came to light as I researched the details of the story Mom told.

Unflattering details? Yes, there are. I am told that such flaws are what make us human and that sharing them reminds us that we are not alone.

– Faith Fisher

Reflections

I recall very vividly storming out of our house on Berry Street in Winnipeg on a particular day. I was somewhere between the ages of eight and ten. I don't recall what prompted it, but there was something going on in the house between Mom and Dad which was beyond my understanding, and whatever it was, it caused me to storm out of the house. Stomping  angrily down the front steps, I turned toward the house and kicked the foundation in a fit of fury, shouting, "Who are these people?! Why was I born into this stupid family?!"

Reflecting on that particularly vivid memory of a childhood tantrum, I now realize why History became my absolute favourite subject in school. What I had experienced developed in me a deep-seated desire to learn and understand the world that I lived in and the people with whom I lived. The life events that impacted and shaped who they had become, as well as placing those events within the scope of broader world events, formed my awareness. Excelling in the subject, I learned about the macro environment in which my parents lived, including events such as the Great Depression and World War Two.

Over the years, I also gained clarity into the micro details of their life, the gains and losses and the impacts those had on me and my siblings. I gained increasing appreciation for Mom's fortitude and her ability to manage difficult realities for the benefit of her family.

– Frank Hay

11

I was sixty-two ears old when I began some serious reflection on my life in the context of the life of my parents.

In the wee hours of a morning in April 2015, I recorded some thoughts about my mom. Although she might have had reason to become angry and bitter over some of the events of her past over which she had little or no control, that is not what  happened. She became an overcomer in a quiet way, with compassion and understanding. In her later years within the community in which she then lived, she was often referred to as an "Angel of Mercy."

Mom's Christian faith was important to her. As I write this, I am watching a commercial artist painting a store window with great creativity. I note that she has the right tools and a steady hand. I think that may have been true of Mom as well. She had the right tools of faith, friends and a desire to serve, and she was steadied by her faith in the Christ whom she depended on.

On that early April morning, I outlined Mom's life as in a ledger. One side of the ledger contained the life event, and on the other side was the loss she sustained. As you read the story, I think you will see for yourself how such a ledger pertains to the events of the life she recorded.

Through research done while putting Mom's story in order, I discovered that she herself did not know "the whole story." It might have been that she simply did not want to know, or perhaps her life was just too full of raising her family and keeping our home life running as smoothly as possible amidst the chaos. I believe the latter.

You will notice that very little is said in this book about the five children she birthed and raised or the illnesses she herself suffered through. To be fair, at age eighty-two, she spent a week rehearsing and recording about thirty-five years of her life. By the point that the recording ends, she was mentally and emotionally exhausted.

I wouldn't say that Mom's life after the end of the story she told was carefree. Raising children and teens on her own would not have been a picnic. She lived the stuff of life and then some.

– Faith Fisher

Crystal M. Hay, 1978

Background

Grandfather Joseph Sloane

My maternal grandfather, Joseph Lesley Sloane, was born July 5, 1884, the second youngest in a family of eleven boys and two older sisters. All were born on a farm in Leamington, Ontario, to Isabella (Fox) and James Thornton Sloan. As was common in that era, the older children presumably helped with raising the younger ones.

James Thornton and Isabella Sloan, circa 1862

It may be noted that my grandfather's parents' last name ends with the letter "n." The letter "e" was added to their children's surname at the turn of the century. The reason is unknown.

Joseph's father died around age fifty, having been accidentally poisoned by potassium nitrate, commonly known as saltpetre, which back then was used as fertilizer and rocket propellant, among other things. Joseph was then about six years old. When he was fourteen years old, their house burned to the ground, and a new one was built. His mother, Isabella, died one month before Joseph turned nineteen.

Grandfather's brother Garfield, two years older, accepted a government offer to homestead and moved west to Cayley, Alberta, about fifty miles south of Calgary. My grandfather, Joseph, followed. It was said that my grandfather did not like the loneliness of farming and didn't do very well. Apparently, he spent a lot of time in the nearby town and a lot of that time in the pool hall.

Garfield, however, did quite well and remained in Cayley until his death in 1950.

Grandmother Mabel Alda Smith

My grandmother, born Maybelle Alda Smith, was only ever known as Mabel. Her parents, John Henry Smith and Charlotte (Johnson), both from Ontario, married and had four children, all born in Cottam in Essex County, Ontario. The Smith family would come to include Frederick Erdmann, Mabel Alda, Cecil Herbert and Bertha Eva. The family eventually moved to Anadarko, Oklahoma, and many of the young family's growing up years were spent there. The Smiths, also enticed by the offer of a homestead in Canada, eventually moved to a farm near

John Henry and Charlotte Smith, circa 1890

what would a few years later be known as the town of Vulcan, Alberta, east of Cayley.

Reid Hill

In 1906, a man named Oric Reid[1] opened a store eleven kilometres east of Vulcan. The following year, the North-West Mounted Police established a temporary post nearby. Reid's homestead was on a large hill,

The Smith Family Homestead

[1] hhttps://www.geocaching.com/geocache/GC7A936_v2v-reid-hill-cemetery-memorial
https://www.postalhistorycanada.net/php/StudyGroups/Alberta/content/JAPH-8.pdf

so the road east of Vulcan became known as the Reid Hill Road. Two years later, Reid moved his general store to the Reid Hill Road. The store also served as the local post office. Mail and the local newspaper arrived every Friday from the nearby town of Stavely. Therefore, Fridays became a social occasion for folks from the country to gather, talk and shop while picking up their mail and newspaper. The "folk from the country" would have included the Smiths and the Sloanes. The general store burned down in 1937.

There was a graveyard in the area as well. People had been buried there from 1895 to 1935. Over time, the graveyard was neglected. Years later, the headstones of the Reid Hill Cemetery were gathered into one corner of the farmer's field along the highway. Unfortunately, many graves were not marked.

Reid Hill Cemetery

The Reid Hill Baptist Church started having services in the Reid Hill School in 1908 and eventually built their own church building. It is not recorded where the little

Reid Hill Baptist Church Dedication 1918

congregation met prior to meeting in the school. It was in that church that Joseph Sloane and Mabel Smith met. They were married in Cayley, Alberta, December 10, 1907. Joseph was twenty-three, and Mabel would turn twenty-three on the 26th of that month.

The graveyard, the general store/post office and the church are the only buildings Mom could remember.

The Alberta Years: Setting a Pattern

It is unclear which years Joseph and Mabel lived in which place. What is clear is that they started their family and remained in Alberta for fifteen

Joseph and Mabel Sloane

years before moving to Winnipeg, Manitoba. Their two oldest children, Charlotte Marie (who was called Marie) and Jasper Lloyd (who was called Lloyd), entered the world in Cayley, Alberta. The family lived both on a homestead and in town. Bertha Smith, Mabel's youngest sibling, was present when Charlotte was born in June 1909. Jasper, who would grow to take on many of the physical attributes of his father, was born December 5, 1911. Cecil Byron joined the little family on October 2, 1913, but died in the Edmonton Hospital the following year at ten months old. In the years 1913– 1915, the family is

Lloyd, Crystal and their mother Mabel near Vulcan, Alberta, 1923

said to have lived in four different homes in Edmonton.

Cecil, however, was buried at Reid Hill Cemetery. On February 14, 1916, Mom (Crystal Myrel) was born in Bawlf, Alberta, in one of the two homes the family occupied there at different times. This little-known community is eighty miles southeast of Edmonton.

Mom recalled having "a wild and wonderful time on the farm near her Smith grandparents' homestead between the ages of five and seven." Family records also indicate that they lived in seven

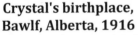

Crystal's birthplace, Bawlf, Alberta, 1916

separate places in Calgary, most likely between 1917 and 1920. It was probably during this time, that my grandfather, Joseph, was believed to have "managed the national system of baking." It is also believed that he sold insurance. At one time, he was "selling silverware up in the mountains for about three months."

While living in Calgary, Joseph had a Model T Ford with side curtains and a top stretched over a framework of wood, just in case it rained. Mom recalled the time a strong whirlwind blew the covering off. My grandfather felt embarrassed while driving around in a frame of woodwork. Eventually, he found the covering in a farmer's field and had it repaired, so his vehicle "looked quite smart again." Calgary was also the place where the family had their first telephone.

Joseph's Model T Ford

Crystal, age 4

It is again on the record that the family lived in two places in Vulcan. Adding it all up, Mom's parents moved their family around Alberta, occupying seventeen different homes—and had four children—in nine years.

Winnipeg, Manitoba

As Mom recorded, her father was "living a lifestyle not approved by one of his relatives." This is believed to have

Marie, Crystal and Lloyd at the Smith homestead

Marie, Crystal and Lloyd, 1922

been Mabel's sister, Bertha, who was constant in her criticism of him. Whatever the reason, Joseph would eventually move to Manitoba, taking with him Mabel and the three surviving children.

Lloyd, with dark hair and eyes, would have been thirteen when they moved. Marie, fifteen, was six-and-a-half years older than Mom, who was seven when they left Alberta. It was said that Marie looked more like Mabel's side of the family and Mom looked like her father's side.

Bertha Myrtle Belle, or Betty, as she came to be known, was born in Winnipeg in 1925, making her nine years younger than Mom.

Mom's two sisters had brown eyes and brunette hair. Mom and her dad were the only ones in the family who had blonde hair and blue eyes. Mom said she often felt like "the little fairy thing" in the middle.

For reasons unknown, in her storytelling, Mom said very little about her own mom. My grandmother kept a scrapbook of articles dating back to 1930 on political and religious leaders and events, along with quotes and poetry from the Bible, newspapers and other publications. She also included birth, death and marriage announcements, as well as greeting cards. Grandmother was obviously aware of world and local events and had a Christian faith. My oldest brother Dan referred to her as being "a little spitfire."

What follows is Mom's story as she told it, beginning with the move to Winnipeg.

PART TWO

MOM'S STORY

1
Elementary School Years

The first place we lived at in Winnipeg was on the second floor of 624 Sherbrook Street. It had a little gas stove. There were just three of us children, Marie, Lloyd and me. Betty had not been born yet. My eighth birthday was celebrated here when my father was away. I attended grade two at Somerset School, which was at 775 Sherbrook Street. Twin girls came to my birthday, and I remember that we played a child's game we called "Mother, May I."

624 Sherbrooke St

444 Maryland

We moved to 444 Maryland Street, but only stayed there a few nights. My father was still away most of the time. Maybe he was still "selling silverware up in the mountains." My mother got a job working at Eaton's department store downtown on Portage Avenue.

We moved again, this time to 585 Ashburn Street,[2] and, not long after that, to 606 Sanford Street. There was a wooden subway on Portage Avenue that streetcars went through, and there was a creek near Polo Park—Omand's Creek. The driver of the streetcar was by the front door, and there was a man at the back to help passengers out the back doors. It was common that when the streetcar went through the subway, the trolley would come off the wire, and everything would black out until the man at the back would get out and hook the wire up again. I had to cross the bridge that went over Omand's Creek to go to Isaac Brock School. By now, I was in grade three.

585 Ashburn

I think that from Sanford Street our next move was to Sharpe Boulevard. The trolley that ran from what was then Pine Street would go a long way around and come out by Sanford Street, where there were three large houses that were all built by the same builder. The Polo Park Race Track was also being built then (1925), and one of the men working on that project boarded at our place on Sharpe Boulevard. Moorgate Street, not far from Sharpe Boulevard, was the end of the city line. Somewhere on this line, there was a wooden bridge, constructed with white boards. Back then, passengers had to buy zone cards to transport them into different zones. It was even possible to get a bus out to Headingley. Portage Avenue then was a two-way street. Trolley buses driving along Portage Avenue would have

---

[2] On February 23, 1926, while the family was at the Ashburn address, Joseph signed a contract with the Northwest Funding Company in Spokane, Washington, to sell on commission the "Law Course" put out by the American Extension University of Los Angeles.

bushes and branches hitting the windows as they went along.

We left Sharpe Boulevard and moved to 566 Camden Place. I think Betty was born while we lived there. There is a

picture of her sitting among the nasturtiums at our Camden Place house when she was six months old. While we lived there, Marie made me a lovely brown coat. I used to sit on the front steps so that everyone could see my nice new coat. Marie was a great seamstress.

Betty at 566 Camden Place

From Camden Place, our family moved once again, to Elmhurst Road. Betty learned to walk while living here. The move during the month of May meant that I had to finish my last two months of school at Isaac Brock School, which meant taking the streetcar.

I had a Miss McGoogin as my teacher in grade three. I remember looking out the school window at the branches on the trees in the spring covered with little brown bumps. The teacher asked a question about them. I replied, "I think the leaves come from those little brown bumps." The teacher asked the class if they thought I was correct. I was embarrassed, and it made me feel unsure. The teacher cast a shadow of doubt, and it really annoyed me.

I also remember practising a folk dance for a spring concert at the school with nine or ten other girls. However, I had moved across the river to Elmhurst Road by then, and I had to take a "stupid" streetcar to Academy Road and transfer. It took me a long time to get to school, and I had to take a lunch.

27

Dad, at that time, was selling *The Book of Knowledge* encyclopedia out in the country. I remember coming home from school one day very hungry. Canned tomatoes had been used to make a sandwich for my lunch. It tasted like plaster. Both Marie and I both threw our lunches in the garbage that day.

I loved to dance and had mimicked another dancer's routine until I knew it well. I was asked to perform it at a school in Sturgeon Creek. My mother insisted that I wear bloomers under my dress and garters to keep them up and "hidden." But, when I began dancing on the stage, which was higher than the audience, a grade six boy, Ed Zoppa, yelled out, "I can see suspenders!"

We lived on Elmhurst Road for a while. By that time, Marie was fifteen years old and worked part-time selling soaps on the main floor in Eaton's. The product Neet (for the removal of underarm and leg hair for women) had been introduced into the market. Marie told the story of an employee's brother who tried to use it to remove his moustache. Another of Marie's friends was so disgusted with the product that she threw it out the second story window. It landed on the tin roof and began to smell after a long time sitting in the sun.

2
Middle School Years

The family moved a few more times before my father would finally be able to buy a house instead of renting. By the time I was eleven, we had already lived in a few houses in the west end of the city. I attended Greenway School while we lived at 600 Banning Street.

Crystal, age 12

The summer after I turned twelve, I remember living in a furnished house at 749 Lipton Street for a couple of months while the owners were away. My Uncle Garfield came to visit while we lived there.

600 Banning

250 Simcoe

When the owners returned, we moved to 250 Simcoe Street. That place was like a barn. I remember I was helping my dad set up beds, and I asked him when we were going to have our first barn dance. He laughed. I think by that time he was starting to mellow. Like a barn, that place was ice cold. We couldn't stand it.

I never had a bicycle, but my brother Lloyd had a good one, and I was able to ride it. I would ride down to Garfield Street near Sargent Avenue and all the way over to Thompson Drive in Sturgeon Creek.

393 Thompson Dr.

We moved once again, to 393 Thompson Drive. I had my thirteenth birthday while we lived there. It was a beautiful home.

Crystal, age 13, at a C.G.I.T. event at Hillside Beach

I started going to the United Church out in Sturgeon Creek. Mrs. Williams was my teacher at C.G.I.T. (Canadian Girls in Training)—we called ourselves "see-jits." I used to sing in the choir, too. There was a fellow there called Ron Patterson,[3] a really a nice boy. His dad had a big rink, and I used to go skating there. Ron used to walk home with me and carry my skates. He was a bit shorter than I was and attended Bannatyne School with me.

Boys and Bikes

In the area of our house on Thompson Drive were wooden sidewalks that were three to five feet above the gullies around there. To ride a bike on those sidewalks was

---

[3] The spelling of the last name could not be confirmed from archived school attendance records. An alternate spelling was Pattison.

always risky; I know because I did it one time and went off into a very deep gully. The streets were cement, and it was better to ride the bikes on the cement. My friends, Isabel McDonald and Ethel Merridew, both had girl's bikes. I would sometimes be able to ride one of the bikes of one of the other kids. Ron liked me to ride his bike because he always kind of liked me at that age. He was about thirteen, too.

One time when I had been out riding, I had to go home for some reason. When I was there, Betty, who was now four years old, had woken up from her sleep. My mom said, "Take Betty with you," and so I did. But Betty didn't like me to get on a bike and ride away from her. She would cry, and she didn't want me to go and ride around the schoolyard. It killed all my fun. So, we walked to the schoolyard. I put up with her for a little while, but then decided to walk her back home. I just let her go in the back door.

I saw Lloyd's bike sitting there, so I rode it back to the school. When it was time to come home, I was riding down Thompson Drive. A fellow named Albert Currie joined me. While we were riding and talking together, I heard my dad give an awful, shrill whistle, and I told Albert, "That's my dad. I've got to go." So, I skedaddled back home.

Lloyd, age 17, with his father, 1928

Now, my dad could be a very hysterical, hot-tempered spitfire at times. When he was at home dealing with a young family, he wouldn't listen to reason, and his eyes would sparkle and snap. He got after me because I was riding a boy's bike. The reason he knew that was because Betty had told him. "Whose bike were you

31

riding?" he demanded. That time, I had been riding Lloyd's bike, so I told him that. "Don't you lie to me, girl! Don't you lie to me!" He was so mad because I was on a boy's bike. He thought all boys were maniacs or something. He was cruel. He literally kicked me right there on the kitchen floor. I don't think my dad realized at that time how unreasonable he could be. I was devastated by the way he was at those times. I think he had business deals or house deals on his mind, and he couldn't stand any interruption in his thinking. Anyway, he forbade me to ever ride on a boy's bike again.

I was on a girl's baseball team then while attending Bannatyne School in grade six. I loved it! We played and practised on a big field. Boy, could I hit that ball! I hit such home runs! But I hated being a fielder because I couldn't stand catching the ball. My dad and mom never came to see our baseball games. I think it was an unheard-of thing at that time. Dad had bigger issues on his mind that were always pressing on him. Sometimes, we had to play against another team. Sturgeon Creek would play against St James. There were older guys who could drive, and sometimes they would take all of us girls in the back of their truck down to play in St. James.

Often, my dad was quite late coming home from downtown, and supper wasn't always ready that early. One girl wanted me to come with her to a game, and so she waited for me to have a bite of supper. Then, these two boys gave us a ride on the handlebars of their bikes. My mom knew about it, but I was scared to death that I would meet my dad along the way, riding on that boy's bike. That worried me all the way there. But we didn't meet my dad, and I heaved a sigh of relief!

I had a close friend named Florence Humphrey. She wasn't on the baseball team. She was a nice girl. We would hop on the old streetcar and go to the Cornish Baths downtown. There was an Arlington streetcar that went across Portage Avenue, right down to what is now the Maryland Bridge. It was an old wooden bridge with cars going both ways. The Cornish Baths were beside the Cornish library in Westgate. We two used to go on Saturdays and have a very good time. Just outside the Baths, there was always a man who sold buttered popcorn out of his orangey-red truck. We would buy some, and then we'd get on the Sherbrook streetcar and go down to Portage Avenue to transfer to another streetcar and go all the way out to Sturgeon Creek. We had to pay the zone fare to get out there.

Girls and Parties

Crystal, 17, and Marie, 24, 1933

My sister Marie remembers all the parties I had. Marie didn't have parties. Lloyd was always out and away. I used to cause my dad grief to no end because I was young and pretty and had a lot of fun. And he couldn't stand me to be with boys. But I had boys at my parties, and I think my dad eventually got used to it.

Betty, age 16, 1941

My mother said I should invite Florence Humphrey to my party, even though I was with a different group of girls and fellows from other parties. Florence wasn't petite and cute in the way that boys of that age seemed to like. She just didn't seem have that "appeal." But I needed to invite her, and she came. At the party, we played Postman's Knock, a naughty game. I had a whale of a time when I was young. We had a closet by the front door in the vestibule, and someone would go in there and call out a number. This guy named Burt Aikenley said to me, "If I call Humphrey's number, you let me know!" I still remember her number was fourteen—I haven't forgotten that to this day. Well, he called fourteen, and I just didn't have the heart to say anything. Florence went in. I didn't know what to do. I thought for sure he wouldn't kiss her. When he came out, he was very angry!

There was another girl I liked but felt sorry for. Her name was also Florence, Florence Narranay. She always looked unwell. I wondered if she had had TB. One day at school, I found a note in my desk: "We wish that you wouldn't hang around with Narranay and Humphrey." It was signed by three of the boys. I was only about thirteen years old, and life to me then was full of parties and fun.

In early spring, we moved from 393 Thompson Drive to 846 Ingersoll Street. This was the first house Dad bought. At the time, he was buying and selling houses, like a real estate agent.[4] My mother said it was the first time we had ever spent two Christmases in one house.

846 Ingersoll

Shortly after the move, I had my fourteenth birthday. My friend down the street gave me a very pretty hankie. Lloyd gave me a big chocolate bar. And that was the extent of the celebrations.

---

[4] In 1939, Joseph Sloane was listed as the Manager of Manitoba Lands located at 207–265 Portage Avenue, Winnipeg. In 1954, he was listed as a real estate agent. Other years, there was no listing of his occupation.

No matter where we moved all over the city, I and my siblings attended Broadway First Baptist Church. Eileen Eastwood, who lived on Valour Road, was in the same Sunday school class as me for years, and we became friends. Sometimes, Eileen and I would go to each other's house for supper. She had some friends who would go to the Berean Church, which was located beside the General Wolfe School on Burnell Street, so sometimes I would go there, too.

We really liked our Sunday school teacher, Mrs. MacDonald. She would have us come to her house away out on Moorgate Street.[5] There were only two houses on Moorgate at the time. The MacDonald family lived in the big one at the end, a huge, three-story house. They used to invite many of the church people to come for corn roasts. We had a lot of fun out there.

There were quite a few kids in the MacDonald family, but Ethel was the one who was more my age. Sometimes, I would go and spend a night out there and sleep between Ethel and her sister, Ivy, the three of us in the same bed. I wouldn't sleep too well.

When Ness Avenue was just bush, farms and dairies, a girl named Ethel Merrydew lived away out there on a farm. One night, rather than one boy walking her home, a whole bunch of us, including my friend, Kathleen, walked her home at 10:30 at night to be sure she got home safely. My dad nearly flipped. No matter how I explained it to him, it didn't matter. My dad gave me a dressing down because I was so late. I think I was going on fourteen at the time. My dad said that the next time I had to be home by eleven o'clock.

The next party I went to was a farewell for Ron Patterson because he was moving to Moose Jaw, Saskatchewan. I was invited because I was his girlfriend. All of the others at the party were sixteen years or older because his sister was sixteen. They were just starting to eat around 11:00 p.m., but I said I had to get home. They begged

---

[5] The Henderson Directories for 1929 and 1930 list "MacDonald" at 310 Moorgate.

me to stay longer. I told them my dad said I *had* to be home by eleven. So, Ron walked me home. He used to write me letters after he moved away.

3
Meeting Bill:
The Developing Friendship

Prior to meeting Bill,[6] I was in grade eight at General Wolfe School and was in the choir. General Wolfe School put on a play called *The Banishment of Rosalind*, taken from Shakespeare's *As You Like It*. The grade nine students were in the play. The grade eight choir sang before the performance and then sat with the audience. I remember seeing a young man there and thinking, "Isn't he handsome looking?!" I was at that age when you take note.

During the play, an old man came on stage. He had a crook in his hand. He was the slave of the prince and said, "Good morning, master." He talked just like an old man even though he was a student. He was terrific at acting. The "old man" turned out to be Bill Hay, but I didn't know him then. I didn't meet him until I was in grade nine at Daniel McIntyre School.

When I was fifteen and in grade eight at General Wolfe School, I first met Marj Bailey. It was at her home the next year where I met Bill Hay. It happened this way. On the first day of September when I was in grade nine, Marj, who had to repeat grade nine, invited me over to her place. She had been talking about a certain fellow whom I happened to know, and she said, "Come on over to my place tonight." I said I would have to see if my friend, Margaret Stewart, would want to go, too. Margaret and I had talked about doing something together that evening, and I didn't want to

---

[6] Bill's legal name is Francis William Hay. It was common that the name Frank was used instead of the name Francis, and Bill instead of the name William.

run out on my own without her. In the end, the two of us went and spent the evening.

There was a fellow there with a guitar. We had been singing when we heard whistling outside. Marj looked and said, "Oh, there's Crosbie and Bill." She called to them, and two boys came in. One was Crosbie McDonald, and the other was Bill Hay. To this point, I had only seen Bill in the play the year before.

I was sitting on a chair in the corner of the room, and there was a hassock by me. Bill sat on the hassock, and Margaret Stewart, Crosbie and Marj sat across the room, and we just chatted. I was not particularly keen on this upstart of a young man who was sitting beside me. He was too quick with his answers and his talk. I was a slow thinker and a slow talker, and he was the opposite. So, I wasn't taken with him because I thought he was too smart.

When Margaret and I decided it was time to go home, all of them decided to walk home with us. Marj Bailey lived at 670 Simcoe Street, between Wellington and Notre Dame, and I lived at 846 Ingersoll Street, which was between Ellice and Sargent. Margaret lived near me. So, all of us—Marj, Bill, Cosbie, Margaret and I—laughed and talked all the way home, although it wasn't very far. We were just a bunch of giggly kids, laughing and talking.

The next time I met Bill and Crosbie, it was because Marj and I played a silly trick. We were just stupid kids. Because Marj liked Crosbie, we wrote a fake invitation to Crosbie and Bill to come over to Margaret Stewart's house. Of course, we didn't say anything to anybody else. On the given day, Marj and I were sitting on Margaret's front steps, and we saw these two guys coming down Ingersoll Street. They were dressed up in hockey sweaters, and they just looked sharp. They had not looked that sharp the first night we had seen them. They appeared to be feeling pretty chipper about the fact that they had been "invited." Anyway, we talked for a bit and then went for a walk. What else did you do in those days?

By this time, Bill now knew where I lived. We weren't together much then, but he had come over one night. I didn't have an English literature book, but he had one. I had an English teacher named Acheson or something who taught us composition, grammar, spelling and literature. I needed a book, and he agreed to help by lending me his. So, it was arranged that Margaret would walk from where she lived and Bill from where he lived, and they would meet. He would give his literature book to Margaret, and Margaret would bring it to me so I could do some composition homework, and then I'd send it back. He did that for a while.

Bill and I were never close friends at that time; we were just friends. If I was at Marj's, I would meet him there. Marj was keen on Crosbie, and Margaret Stewart liked Crosbie, too. We'd all get together, just a bunch of young people. We'd go skating sometimes or tobogganing. Bill was a good skater. He played hockey on a local team even after he was through high school.

A lot of the friends that I had known over the previous years out in Sturgeon Creek were going to have a wiener roast at City Park.[7] I was invited to come and bring a friend. By now, Bill and I had been friends for a period of time, and so Bill came with me. Ron Patterson, who had once lived out in Sturgeon Creek and had moved to Moose Jaw, Saskatchewan, had written me a letter. I took the letter with me to the wiener roast, and I let the kids read it. Ron was a nice fellow and used to write easy letters.

On Ingersoll Street, I had a Halloween party with my friends from back in Sturgeon Creek, including Burt Aikenley and Jim Brown. When they knocked on the door, I nearly split my sides! Their mothers must have helped them get dressed. One had a pink shirt with a big blue bow under his neck, and the other had a blue shirt with a big pink bow. Their mothers had curled their hair and put makeup on

---

[7] This park was commonly referred to as City Park until it was eventually and officially named Assiniboine Park.

them, and they were acting like they were two sissies. We had such fun at that party!

There was another knock on the door, and there were three guys that I didn't recognize. They had sideburns and looked like they were twenty-year-olds. They called out "Halloween apples!" I thought, "What on earth are these adults doing collecting Halloween apples?" But when I looked closer, I realized it was Dave Williams and two of his friends who were dressed as The Three Musketeers. What a howl we had that night!

There was another guy named Jimmy Pringle who used to go to the church, and he came to the party, too. He used to walk me home from the church young people's group sometimes. I was a "dumb bunny." He said to me one time, "You know, I've been so absent minded since I met you." I said to him, "What an insult!" I had no knowledge of the modern talk and that I should have taken it as a compliment.

4
High School

Bill was a hockey player. He was on a local team and continued to play after he graduated from high school. He finished school a year before me. I was going to Broadway Baptist Church, and he would say that he would meet me at the church, but then he would go and play hockey instead. I

remember that. He played hockey a lot. I wasn't very gracious. I thought he should come to church and not play hockey.

Eventually, it got to the point that Bill would go to the church service at Broadway First Baptist. I'd sing in the choir, and he'd sit

Crosbie and Bill, best friends

in the balcony. Afterward, we'd go home together and have a snack at my house, and then he'd go home. For the first year or two, that's the way it was.

Once, Crosbie came to pick me up because the puck

had hit Bill in the lip during a hockey game, and he had to go

41

and have it stitched. We were invited out to a Sunday dinner at some friends of his folks that day, and all he could do was suck some food through a straw. He had a fat lip.

My sister, Marie, now age twenty-three, married Harold Newman on June 1, 1932, in that house at 846 Ingersoll Street. I was sixteen. My father had cut my hair, but he had cut it too short and left a mess at the back. I had to wear a ribbon around my head to cover up the imperfections. At the wedding, I played the piano, and Marj sang. She had a lovely voice.

When I turned seventeen, we were then living in the Belrose Apartments[8] at the corner of Lipton Street and Wolseley Avenue. From here, it was a long walk to get to school.

Belrose Apartments

Crystal, age 17

I had to walk from the Belrose Apartments down to Westminster Avenue, to Portage Avenue, to St. Matthews Avenue, to Ellice Avenue, to Sargent Avenue, and finally to Wellington.

By this time, I was becoming self-conscious about Bill coming over. We'd had a friendship for quite a while. On my birthday, Bill brought me a beautiful fountain pen and pencil set, and a jigsaw puzzle. Maybe he brought me chocolates, too—he

---

[8] These were built in 1914 and are currently known as Bellarosa Apartments.

used to bring me things. That very cold February night, after Bill had gone home, I started working on the jigsaw puzzle. I finished it just in time to go to school the next day!

There was one time when Marj, Crosbie, Bill and I went out to City Park. The wires of the trolley came off, and the lights went out. Marj and Crosbie teased Bill and me saying, "We saw what you were doing while the lights were out!"

One time when Marie had come to visit, Bill came over to visit me. I had put a dress on, and I asked Marie if my slip was showing. She said, "Oh, no. It's alright...Why don't you ask Bill?" We left that room and went into the living room, where Harold and Bill were sitting. Marie said, "Bill, Crystal was asking me if you could see...the Northern Lights in the summertime." She was always teasing me.

Bill was in grade eleven while I was in grade ten. He had a good voice and was in the play *Pirates of Penzance*. But I don't think his family ever took church and school activities very seriously. They never came to watch him.

I remember Bill going to the young people's group with me at Broadway Baptist Church and then coming home and having a cup of tea or something. Marie said she liked Bill because "he was always so jolly and so full of fun." He was just like one of our family. It seemed he was always coming over to our place. Mom and Dad were getting to know him, but I don't think they drew any real conclusions during that time. They thought he was just a fellow who came over to help me with homework.

Although Bill was always welcome in our home, I remember my dad getting a little annoyed at the fact that Bill was always coming over to our place and yet I never went to Bill's place. I did, but only on occasions such as New Year's Day or something. Dad used to say things such as, "Is he ashamed of you or something? What's the matter with that family? Why do you never go to their place?" I don't know whether Dad should have said all those things, but he used to get carried away with his thoughts.

Of course, there *was* something wrong at our place. We were living in that little Belrose apartment at the time. I mentioned all of this to Bill, and I guess his family decided that he'd better have me over. And so I went. Each time, his mom would put out her best china, and I got to know the family a bit more.

Marie and Harold used to come to our little apartment on Sunday for dinners, but then they moved to Windsor, Ontario. However, Harold's father still lived in Winnipeg, and we had him come for Christmas dinner. We served rice because it was cheap.

Leaving School

We lived in the Belrose Apartments until Dad couldn't pay the rent and the gas bill. The bailiffs were going to be sent over to take whatever stuff he had, which wasn't much. But Dad asked a guy named Jim MacDuff from Sturgeon Creek to be there at 5:00 a.m. We got away before the bailiffs came.

All of this was hard on my mother. My mom used to accuse my dad of just "playing house" and not knowing how to really run a house.

From the Belrose, we moved to a place on Greenacre Street.[9] At some point, my dad had bought that property for ten dollars per acre. He wanted to put a fence around about an acre of that land, and he got me to help him. He had a post hole auger. He would get the first fence post in, and he'd have me hold the fence post. He'd say, "Now a little to the right. Now just a little to the left. Now just a little to the right...Hold it there!" Then he'd come and put the earth back in around the post while I held it. We had to do that for every post. We planted a big garden there, including strawberries.

I didn't go back to school after grade ten. I had been in the commercial course at Daniel McIntyre High School,

---

[9] Now known as Greenacre Boulevard in Kirkfield Park, this is now a fully developed residential area.

taking Typing. But this course was only offered in city schools. From Greenacre Boulevard, I had to have a zone ticket to get to the city limits and then a streetcar ticket to get to Daniel McIntyre, and we didn't have car fare. The only high schools closer were St. James Collegiate, which didn't teach commercial, or St. Charles High School, which would have been like going to a convent. I couldn't have afforded to get to St. James Collegiate, even if they had had a commercial program, because we were outside the city limits.

On the last day of school at Daniel McIntyre, I had to go back to get my report card. The report cards wouldn't be handed out until the afternoon, and that day I hadn't any lunch. A girl named Clara invited me to her house so I could have something to eat. And that was the end of my schooling.

That winter, my dad called himself "The Human Snowmobile." He would walk in snow up to his hips to bring in live chickens to kill them, stick them, dress them and then sell them so he could bring home some money for food. He often came to me for money for this or that. Those were very hard days.

Old Man Newman, as I called him (Marie's father-in-law), was a contractor and had a business building bridges and docks, and I guess he made some money to keep his business running. He had an old Dodge half-ton truck that he didn't use, and he let my dad use it. That was a good thing because now Dad had something to get around town in. You could buy gas for nineteen cents a gallon. I think he made enough for gas by selling chickens. Everything was cheap then. There were some places you could go to get food given to you when there was an overload of something.

A Long-Distance Relationship
In 1933, I was seventeen and living out on Greenacre. When I met Bill, I had been only fifteen, so we had been friends for a couple of years. He would come out to

45

Greenacre once in a while if he had car fare. One time, he walked out because he didn't have any. He would come in an evening, and we would go for a walk because we had nothing else to do.

One afternoon early in September, he came and told me that he'd be going away sometime soon to find work. When Bill's parents had thought they were going to lose their house, they had rented it out instead. That summer, they had had the furniture packed up, and Bill's mom had taken his sister Cora back east, to Toronto, which is where they were

Bill's family home, 667 Toronto Street

from. Bill's oldest sister, Gertie, had a steady job with the Wiggins System, which had to do with licence plates. Bill's dad did furniture finishing and still worked through the next winter. His dad and Gertie moved into two rooms on Furby Street. I think they thought that Bill wouldn't be able to find work and would have to come and live with them, too. Instead, Bill went east. It wasn't until years later that Bill told me that he "rode the rails" out east. He was embarrassed to tell me some things. He went with another young man, and when the other man said he was ready to go, Bill

Gertie, age 7, and Bill, age 3, 1918

had to go right then. That's what men did in those days. They'd hop the freight trains to go to another place to try to get work, because they had no money to go as paying passengers as Bill's mother had done with Cora.

Bill was eighteen when he left in September 1933. Before he left, he gave me a little teapot that looked like a little cottage with a blue door. I still have it.

In October, I started a job as a live-in nursemaid over in Tuxedo, two streets from City Park, on the other side of the river from where we lived. It was a nice home, and I looked after the Roberts family's children.

Bill used to write me letters all the time from Toronto. Sometimes, I'd get as many as three letters in a week. The postman who delivered the mail was a little bit of a man. For some reason, he began to call me the heavy lover. I got a bang out of that.

I had my eighteenth birthday the next February, and Bill sent me a birthday card and a present. It was slippers with fur around the edges. Somehow, he'd gotten the idea that I was his kitten, and on the card he had written, "You're my kitten, and a kitten needs fur."

Bill had been away for at least six months. I guess the times were no better out east in the beginning of those Depression years. We were all thinking that things would pick up, but they didn't. However, Gertie didn't lose her job, and Bill's dad still had his work, so the family all came back again. Because they'd rented their house out, they had to find another place to live for a while. Bill's mother, Gertie and Cora rented a couple of rooms, and then they found an apartment suite on Kennedy, south of Portage, the Astoria Apartments, I think.

Bill had just got back to the city, and he wanted me to come up to the apartment. When I arrived, he opened the door and gave me a big hug and a kiss. We didn't used to kiss before then, but this was special—he'd just got back, and they'd been out east for the whole winter. Eventually, Bill's family moved back into their house.

Bill began to visit me again. If I was at home, but had to go to work in Tuxedo, he'd come out to my house and then go with me to work. He'd leave me there and go home.

5
Harcourt Street:
Getting Married

We finally left our place on Greenacre Boulevard and moved to 202 Harcourt Street,[10] and we lived there quite a while. It, too, was away out in the sticks in Kirkfield Park. Bill would walk miles to come and see me in those Great Depression days when he couldn't afford a streetcar ticket.

Not long after the move, my mother had to go east to see her father, who had taken very ill. They thought maybe he was on his deathbed, but he wasn't. My dad wanted me to leave my live-in nursemaid job in order to come home and take care of things there. So, I left that good job with the Roberts family to come home.

Mom went down east in April. My brother Lloyd, by that time, had already gone east to work and was staying with Marie and Harold. He owed me money for a sofa we had bought previously for Dad and Mom, and he finally sent me a cheque for fifteen dollars. I used it to buy a nice swagger suit. Although Mom had gone east "just for the summer," she ended up staying there for six months. It got chilly, and she wrote Dad saying, "I need a coat." Dad couldn't afford to buy her a coat, so I wrapped up my swagger coat and sent it to her. You have no idea how painful that was for me.

Getting to Know Bill's Family

Bill's mom was Irish, and she used to talk about the green land of Ireland. She had a lot of superstitions about fairies and leprechauns. I didn't know much about anything.

---

[10] This is now the site of St. Basil's Ukrainian Catholic Church.

I had a mole on my face, which was supposed to be a lucky sign according to Irish folklore. Bill's mom had a piano, and she used to get me to play "The Flower Song."

Bill's family was very uneducated. I don't think his mother had more than grade two, and I don't think his dad had much education at all, but money...they knew how to get what they could.

Bill's mom used to "play the horses," which I didn't know about at the time. While Bill was overseas, she got clear title to her house because she kept winning playing the horses. They had a nice house, and they always kept it painted.

Bill used to tell me that his father had a furniture finishing shop in the two front rooms of that house, but his dad came home one night, and his mom had cleared out everything.

Elizabeth and Frank Hay with Bill and Gertie, 1915

Bill's father's business cards

I think Bill's dad and mom had bought that house when the First World War began, and they must have bought it when it was brand new. Gertie was born first, in 1911, Bill was born in 1915, and Cora came later, in 1917. They were all born in that house.

When Bill was very young, his Mom, angry with his Dad, went down east with Gertie, leaving Bill with his Dad. That was an unpleasant experience. I don't know what the trouble was. Maybe it had something to do with his dad having his business and big workshop in the house. His dad was quite a drinker, too. Anyway, Bill's mom finally came back home, and Cora was born sometime afterward.

The United Church of Canada

Saint Paul's Church
Winnipeg, Manitoba

CERTIFICATE OF BAPTISM

This is to Certify that _FRANCIS WILLIAM ANDREW HAY_ was this day Baptized by me "Into the Name of the Father, and of the Son, and of the Holy Ghost," and is therefore acknowledged as a Member of the Church, to be brought up in the nurture and admonition of the Lord.

Place and Date of Birth Winnipeg, Manitoba, 27th May 1915.

Father's Name Frank Hay   Mother's Name Elizabeth Sydney

Dated this 23RD day of MARCH 1932.

Certificate of Bill's baptism at age 12

Gertie, Bill and Cora   Frank, Elizabeth, Gertie, Cora and Bill

51

They used to like to play a card game called Euchre, which was new to me. They would have friends in, and they would play their game. I would be there for supper or something, and we would visit for a while. Then Bill would take me home or take me back to work.

There was no real unpleasantness between me and Bill's parents, at least not then. My dad didn't get to know his folks very well, and my mother didn't know them at all. My father was more outgoing than my mother, who was quieter.

Engagement: On and Off and On Again

After Bill had come back from Ontario, we were dating on a regular basis. At least, he used to come out and see me.

I was friends with a lot of girls in those days, and Bill just fit in. But I wasn't always very happy with Bill. He sometimes used to put some of my friends down a bit, including my friend Eileen Eastwood, which I didn't appreciate because they were my friends.

Eileen had a big surprise party for me on my twentieth birthday. I was working away from home at a different live-in place then, but I told the lady of the home, "I've got to be home tonight because I think my friend is going to have a party for me." I had suspicions because Eileen wanted me to be home at a certain time. I did go home, and they did have a surprise party for me. Well, to them it was a surprise. A bunch of young people came out from the city for the party. Eileen, by this time, was going to Westwood Pentecostal Church, and I was still going to Broadway Baptist with my family. She went out a lot with those young people, and some of the Westwood young people came to the surprise party, along with some other friends. But Bill wasn't at that party.

By now, Bill and I had begun to talk about getting married. I must have been nineteen or twenty when that conversation began to come up. Bill was getting to hug me a little more.

I turned twenty-one in February 1937. Marie was expecting a baby in June, so I decided to go down east then to be with her. The night before I left, Bill took me out for dinner at the Kensington Café[11] on Portage Avenue in downtown Winnipeg. When I got there, he had an engagement ring. He didn't want me to go away. That was the night when we formally got engaged.

I went all the way from Winnipeg to Windsor, Ontario, by bus. I had to change buses at Minneapolis and at Chicago. I was only twenty-one and not used to travelling on buses by myself, and it was stressful having to wait five hours in the Minneapolis bus depot for the next bus to arrive. I had my engagement ring, it was a little too big for my finger, and I was constantly worried I was going to lose it.

I got to Windsor and stayed there for a good two months. Marie gave birth to David. I visited with a lot of my dad's relatives and stayed at their homes and did different things while I was there.

There was a fellow named Jack Monahan who was a friend of my brother Lloyd. Lloyd, living in Windsor then, had a car and was going with a girl named Bernadette. So,

---

[11] This was likely the Olympia Café in the Kensington Building at Smith and Portage, erected in 1905.

sometimes Lloyd, Bernadette, Jack Monahan and I would take a drive out in the country. There were a lot of places to stop along the way. At one particular stop, we could have all the buttermilk we wanted to drink for five cents, and in the hot summertime, it tasted good. The four of us went there a few times. Maybe that's why Bill wanted to get engaged before I went.

I returned home. By this time, Bill's dad had helped him to buy an old Essex car for fifty dollars. You could see right to the ground through one of the floorboards. Bill came out to visit one night very excited because he had a car. Sometimes Bill and I would go into town to Bristol's Fish and Chips, which was a treat for us. Then he would take me back home. One time when Bill came to visit, the car needed to have water put in it. My dad had a hard time paying the bills. I was too embarrassed to tell Bill that our water had been cut off, so I said, "Let's go to the filling station and get it filled there." We did, and we then went downtown to the fish and chip shop. Bill surmised that there was something wrong, and he made a comment about my dad not paying his bills. That made me so angry I could have kicked him. I didn't like him making a remark like that about my dad. There were times when I used to get a little huffy, and there was a period of time after we were engaged that I wasn't very happy about things.

Bill had a hard time telling his folks that he wanted to get married. His dad would just say, "Oh, you're a fool," and leave it at that. We would try to set a date, but his mother wouldn't listen to him. He couldn't get through to them.

I mentioned all this to my dad, and he asked me if he should go and talk with Bill's mom. I said, "Well, yes." I was glad about that. So, he went to talk to Bill's mom, and when he came back, he said they had talked about the money part of getting married. Bill's mom had said to my dad, "Well, Bill needs to have about five hundred dollars in the bank before he gets married, and they should wait a couple of years."

Dad also told me, "She wants to talk with you." I said, "Okay." So, I made arrangements to go over and talk with her. Bill would be at work then, at the Hudson's Bay store. When I got there, we talked about the weather and a few other things, and I kept wondering why she didn't talk to me about our getting married. Finally, I said to her, "My dad said you wanted to talk to me."

She said, "Well, yes, Crys." She had a hard time facing issues too, I guess. Then she said that Bill needed to save some money and we should wait for a couple of years. She also suggested that when we did get married, Gertie and Cora would like to have a shower for us. It didn't seem to be the thing to do at that point, as it would normally be done just before the wedding. I think it was a stalling tactic.

Bill had turned twenty-two in May, and I would be twenty-two the next February. I said to her, "Well, I guess we'll talk it over."

When Bill came out the next time, we talked about it. I said that his mom thought we should wait a couple of years. Now, when you're talking about marriage and you're beginning to hug each other, two years is a long time. Bill was caught in the middle. I was a little frustrated that his mother wanted him to keep living with them. She always wanted her family to be paying money into the home. Cora was taken out of school as a young person and was their little housemaid. Bill was working, and Gertie was working, and times were tough. I guess having almost lost their house once, Bill's mom wanted the money. I think that was the basic problem, and Bill seemed to be unwilling to talk about it with them. Maybe she figured that, with Bill living at home, he would keep paying her room and board and not get married. I couldn't understand it, and that's when I think I got upset. I gave him back his ring and said, "Look, your mother wants you to do so and so. If you want to go and be with your mother, you go." He was kind of annoyed with me and made some comment about going with me all this time

55

and now I wanted to cut it off. He was angry about that, but I was angry too.

We both tried to agree that we should wait two or three years. In Bill's mind, he must have agreed because he didn't persist with setting a date. He wanted to back away and try to appease his mother. This was one of the problems—he was stuck between me and his family so much of the time.

I still had my girl friends and would go to see them. A lot of them lived away out on Beresford Avenue, on Jubilee Avenue, and near River Park. Florence Humphrey and I were still good friends. To get out there, I had to take the old zone streetcar and then the city streetcar, get off at Osborne and Portage, take an Osborne streetcar and then get off at Beresford. We girls used to do all kinds of crazy things together—bonfires and wiener roasts and sing-songs.

I was coming home from one of those times, and the streetcar I needed was up at Eaton's. In those days, the streetcar would drive in the middle of the road and there were safety railings that would fence you in while you waited for one. Bill told me afterward that he was in a car with a bunch of guys and he spotted me. But I had changed my mind and, instead of waiting by Eaton's, I decided I would walk down to the Hudson's Bay store and catch the streetcar there. So, I left the stand and started walking. Bill got the guys to stop, and he got out of the car and dashed back to the stop by Eaton's, but by that time I wasn't there.

Another time, my mother saw Bill get off a streetcar and said, "Oh, there's Bill." I said, "Don't tell him I'm home." I wasn't too keen on seeing him then.

Eventually, Bill did come back to visit. He, too, was disturbed by his parents' reaction. But when he came to the house, I remember that I was rather cool. I wasn't too anxious to dive into too much at that point. When he left my house that time, the engagement was still off. But Bill kept coming back.

I'm not sure when exactly, but eventually I got the ring back. I don't remember how long it took because I had remained cool for quite a while. Then, when we began to talk again about setting a date, he gave me a lovely cedar chest.

Bill couldn't talk to his folks. His dad simply didn't care, and his mother was strung up all the time to keep the house together financially. So, because of the Depression and because of his folks, we waited quite a long time—but we didn't wait the whole two years.

The Wedding Plan Discussions

We were trying to plan a time when we would get married, but Bill couldn't tell his folks, and the Second World War had just started, in September 1939.

I was working part-time at Eaton's, and Bill was working in the Radio and Appliance Department at the Hudson's Bay store. He had been working there for a while, but he didn't make a big wage. In those days, you didn't make a big wage anywhere. I remember Bill telling me that with the Hudson's Bay Company, if you were married, you earned eighteen dollars a week, a married man's wage. The Hudson's Bay Company frowned on their employees getting married because then they would have to pay them more than the twelve dollars a week Bill was earning as a single man. It's hard to explain to anybody these days what those Depression years were like.

I used to tell Bill all the sad things in my family's life. My folks had had to go on welfare. They called it "Relief" in those days. I was embarrassed to tell Bill. It was too hard. But we had to have something to eat, and it was getting to the point where my dad couldn't make any money. There were no opportunities, as nothing was moving.

It turns out that Bill's folks were also on Relief at the time, but I didn't know that. It was only a while later that Bill finally told me. He would never tell me things like that or volunteer that kind of information—probably because I was always talking. That's how it was in those days. We were young and too embarrassed to say things.

I asked my friend, Francis Graham, if she would be my bridesmaid. I told her about our situation and that no one knew Bill and I were making our plans. I said, "We thought we'd just get married, but we wouldn't tell our folks till we could arrange to get a place together."

She said, "I don't care if you don't tell anybody else in the world, but you tell your mother!"

I thought, "Yeah, I should tell Mom and Dad."

So, I went to my mom and dad and told them that we wanted to get married, but that we couldn't afford to set up a place to live in right away. I asked if I could still live at home for a little while until the two of us could get a place. They realized that Bill was having difficulty with his folks, and so they agreed that it would be alright. After that, we went ahead and planned the wedding. My dad couldn't afford anything for a wedding. Nobody had money.

The Wedding and the Funnymoon

Bill and I went to see Pastor Wescott at Broadway First Baptist Church. Bill was a little nervous about everything that was going on, and I was too. My folks were very poor, and his folks were too, and there was the fear that if he got married, the Hudson's Bay Company would fire him so they wouldn't have to pay him more. Whether they would have or not, I'm not sure. Bill wasn't absolutely sure either, but I don't think he was just using this as an excuse to not get married. It was a reality as far as we knew. So, when we talked to Pastor Wescott, we said, "We want to get married, but we don't want it to be known to everyone because of Bill's job security." We set the wedding for October 25, and we would be married in the little church parlour.

I made my dress and hat. It was October, so I made a beautiful midnight blue velvet dress. It took a little bit of creativity and work, but I had bought a pattern and just enough material. The neck was square, so I bought two little decorative pins and put one in each corner. I made a little hat to go with the dress. In those days, you wore a veil, so I

58

made the hat to fit my head, braided a brim, and then attached it, tacking on the little veil. I had that dress for many years after the wedding.

Francis, my bridesmaid, worked away from home in a live-in situation, but she had a little suite where she lived. I

went to her place to get dressed for the wedding.

We were married in the church parlour. My folks and Betty were there. Crosbie was Bill's best man and brought his girlfriend, Fern.[12] Francis Graham was my bridesmaid. She wished afterwards that she'd brought her boyfriend, but I didn't know all the social conventions and had not thought to include him.

Broadway First Baptist Church, 2022

Following the ceremony, we went to Moore's Restaurant on Portage Avenue and had dinner. Mom and Dad weren't able to come to the dinner. Afterward, Bill took me home, with Betty, to my mom and dad's place. I lived at home for a while, and Bill would come out and stay weekends. What a wedding! What a "funnymoon"!

The Truth Is Out

At some point, Bill's mother became suspicious and asked him, "Are you married?" When he said, "Yes, we are," she knew that he needed to get a place. She had a friend who lived on Home Street, down near Wellington, and she got us

---

[12] The Henderson Directory of 1940 lists Crosbie as salesman at George N. Jackson Ltd., living at 677 McDermot. He does not appear again in the Directory until 1949, when he is listed as Crosbie (Fern), living at 317 Sharpe Boulevard, supervisor at George N. Jackson. It is assumed that Crosbie and Fern eventually got married.

our first two-room suite. We moved there in January or February, and by this time I was pregnant. We began to accumulate some things. We bought two chairs and a second-hand Chester bed that Bill got from the Hudson's Bay store and had delivered.

Bill had a bike, and he would bike to work at the Hudson's Bay store, bike home for lunch, and then bike back to work. But his mom had a hold on him to the point that he would bike over to their home and then bike on to work. It got so that some evenings he would bike over to his parents' place after work. I did not like that, of course.

Crystal and Bill, wedding photo, October 25, 1939

We didn't have a phone, and sometimes Bill's folks would send Cora over with messages. One time, there was some cousin of Bill's coming into the city, and Cora came to ask if Bill would come over that evening to see his cousin. I wasn't asked to come, and I didn't like that. Those are things that got under my skin. They all went out together for a meal and a movie and then came back. Bill was late getting home, and I was really quite annoyed. That's when he pulled out a cigarette and started smoking. I was very angry with myself and thought, "How could I be such a gullible person?"

When we knew that we were going to have the baby, we left Home Street and moved back out to Dad and Mom's on Harcourt Street. That was in the fall, September or October. It was good to be away from the influence of Bill's family all the time and his cousins and his sister Gertie, who could be rather difficult. But this move came to be known as the move to "Hard Times House."

6
Hard Times House

It was a very peculiar year. A lot of those years were peculiar, and I would never want to live through them again. 202 Harcourt Street was a big, three-storey house. Marie was living there with her two children, but Harold had gone off to work in Montreal. They had two large rooms in the front

202 Harcourt Street

of the house, while Bill and I were at the back. Bill and I had the bigger area. We had the Chester bed and two chairs that we had had in that first little house on Home Street. Betty, Mom and Dad lived downstairs.

We had an icebox, and when Bill would come home at noon, he would bring a big block of ice and put it in the icebox, and that's how we kept our butter and milk cold. There was a little, four-burner cookstove, and the coal furnace was in the basement. The chimney that ran up from there gave us heat, so it was cozy.

There were steps up to the top storey to the little room where the commode was, which had to be emptied all the time. Bill had fixed that little room up. He was good in many ways. He ran a pipe up for water and made a stand, like a little cupboard, to put a wash basin in.

One time, we were very short of coal. My dad was worried, Marie was worried, and Bill was worried. We were all worried. When Bill went off to work, Marie ordered some coal, Dad managed to get some coal, and Bill ordered some coal while he was at work. So, we then had enough coal for the rest of the winter! It was a good thing, but we all felt unbelievable pressure to do things.

There was one time when Cora came over and slept with us. I don't know what the problem was, but she didn't want to be alone. She came and spent the night, right between Bill and me on our Chester bed. I liked Cora. She was always sweet, but her life was very difficult. She'd had polio as a young child and never went to school, so, of course, she didn't comprehend many things. She was the go-between when Bill's parents wanted to send a message, unless Bill had stopped in at their place.

My dad was still on welfare, I was pregnant and working part-time at Eaton's. We lived on Harcourt Street all that winter of 1940-41. Times were tough, and everyone was doing what they could.

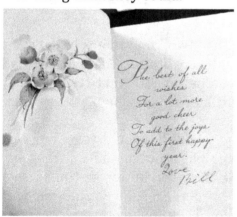 

Our First Baby

Bill was still working at the Hudson's Bay store, and he had the use of a little Austin car. Somebody would have to drain the water out of it at night in the winter, so it wouldn't freeze. On the day I went into labour—the exact due date for the baby's birth—Bill asked if it was it safe for him to go down and take the water out of the radiator of the Austin. I said it seemed like it to me, so he went down to let the water out. I don't know if it was the power of suggestion, but my water broke.

I said to Marie, "Marie, I can't stop peeing."

She realized what was happening. So, someone went over to use the phone at the neighbours' because we didn't have a phone. The doctor said to take me to the hospital.

It was about minus fifteen degrees Fahrenheit. They got a hot water bottle ready and put it in the car, and Bill put the water back in the radiator and got the car warmed up. We had to get from Harcourt Street to River Street down on Osborne, where the old Victoria Hospital was. It was midnight before we got there. Back then, men didn't stay at the hospital when women were giving birth. Bill called his mother to tell her what was happening, and then he went to stay at their place.

I was in labour all that night. I didn't know why I had to have such pain. They gave me ether, and I was half in and half out and didn't know what was going on. I didn't know that there was a problem.

The baby was born at a quarter to ten in the morning. I never heard her cry. I just remember the doctor saying something, and then I thought I heard the word "air." I thought, "Oh, they must be giving her air." I always knew that babies should cry when they were born. I guess the doctor hadn't given me enough ether, and so I felt the last two stitches. They brought me back to a bed in a room and got me settled. That's when the doctor came in and told me the baby was stillborn.

I was still groggy and was seeing double all that day. Believe it or not, the woman in the bed next to me had been the manager of the department where I had been working at Eaton's up until a few days before delivery.

Caesareans were not common in those days. If the baby was out of position, the doctor would try to move the baby into position. Sometimes that worked out pretty well, and sometimes it didn't. They didn't use X-rays, and so they wouldn't know exactly what the position was.

When I was working as a live-in nursemaid at age seventeen, this family had a little girl who was missing two ribs. As that little girl grew, one shoulder grew higher, and her back was getting twisted. She had been turned in her mother before she was born, and they often wondered about that; there were risks in turning a baby.

So, when I was in labour, the idea of doing a Caesarean didn't even seem to cross their minds. The nurse sat there all the time, checking me and watching for the head to emerge. I guess they must have given me something to put me out because I don't remember the doctor coming in. I think they must have phoned him when they realized there were complications. I learned later that her arms had been locked above her head, and she couldn't be born that way. They had to get those arms down before she could be born. I don't know how long it took for the actual birth, but I guess she just couldn't struggle anymore. She came out buttocks first.

Our baby wasn't very big, but she was twenty-two inches long. I blame my dad for that because he was such a tall man and she probably inherited her height from him. I remember that when she started moving during my pregnancy, her head would make my stomach bulge, and the bulge was always in the same place.

I think the doctor suspected there was a problem because he had said to me, "I think that, for your first baby, it is better to be in a hospital than at home because if there are any complications, you have help." I had never had any fear the whole time I was pregnant, so it's a good thing you don't always know what is ahead of you. Anyway, that bump was always the head up there. I had thought that maybe it was the little bum. I didn't know. Because my water had broken the night before, it was a dry birth, which is a difficult one.

It was about a quarter to ten in the morning of November 28 when she was born, and a little while later, Bill came to the hospital from his mother's place. While he was sitting there talking with me and hearing that the baby had been stillborn, one of the nurses came and called him out of the room. He was gone for quite a bit. When he came back, he looked stunned. I can still see the expression on his face. He sat down and didn't say anything.

Finally, I asked, "What did they want you for?"

He said, "Well, they showed me the baby." He was still in a bit of shock.

Later on, when he was able to get his voice back and talk a bit, he said that what had struck him was that this little baby looked exactly like him. He could see it right away, and he couldn't get over it. It amazed him.

I never did see her. I was too groggy, I was seeing double, and...well, I sort of grasped what had happened, but not really. I hadn't seen her, but Bill had, and I think that made the difference with him.

Later that evening, I did ask the nurse if I could see the baby, and she said, "You know they discolour very quickly. They don't always look very nice, and besides, the baby's gone down now, wherever they take them." She was very gentle in telling me, and I accepted what she was saying. They kept you in the hospital for ten days back then.

The Burial and Recovery

The baby was taken to Bardal's Funeral Home, and my family and Bill's family went down to see her. She was then taken to the Brookside Cemetery, where she was buried. Marie told me all about it—how the funeral home did something to put colour back on the baby and about the little, white casket.

I don't remember if Bill's mother came to see me when I was in the hospital that first time, but when the baby was in Bardal's, the only one who would not go and see the baby was Gertie. Bill, still staying at his mom's, would be up and down crying night after that night, and Gertie just said, "What's the matter with you?" She was very hard, as hard as nails. I can't remember if the death of the baby softened Bill's mom.

There was no funeral service, just a burial. That was at the end of November, so there wasn't much that could be done.

We were still living out on Harcourt Street. The family had put all the baby stuff in the attic where I wouldn't see it when I came home from the hospital. We had had a crib and everything.

In early spring, Bill looked around and finally got a flat stone. He had "Baby Hay" and the date engraved on it. I don't know if he wanted to put "stillborn" on it, but he didn't. In May, after the snow was gone, Bill took me down to that little grave for my first time. That's when it hit me.

Bill and I then decided we'd get another place to live. I said to Bill, "Now, were going out to find a place. Let's just you and I go. Don't ask your mother. Let's get something of our own." But we didn't move until the next fall.

7
On Our Own

After this first birth, the doctor gave me some advice. He said I shouldn't have another baby for at least two years after that birth. He told me that you count back fourteen days from when your next period is due, then you add two days on either side of that, that's when you are most likely to get pregnant, and you should avoid anything during that time. Well, I put two more days on either side of that.

I came home and told Marie, and Marie said, "You've got that backwards! That's the only time you can't get pregnant!" She sent me for a loop. I was so upset that I phoned the doctor. I found out she was wrong and I was right—but, lo and behold, in three months, I was pregnant again! Danny was born one year and twelve days after that little girl was born.

At the beginning of the second pregnancy, we moved to 484 Ingersoll Street near Portage Avenue. There was a filling station on the corner, and then there was this house. We had a lovely suite up there, and it was close enough for Bill to ride his bike to work. We moved there in May 1941.

I had gone back to the same doctor, Dr. McGrier, who had taken me through my first pregnancy and delivery. One day, I had Bill's mom over for a visit. There were others visiting too, but I don't remember who. They all knew I was pregnant again, and Bill's mom commented to another person, "Yeah. And she's gone back to the same doctor again, you know." That's the way it was.

In this place that we now were living, we wanted to lay new linoleum in the room at the front. We used it as a living room then.

May 27 was Bill's birthday, and although he had to go to work that day, I had planned that we would have a nice lunch together. However, he phoned me up from work and said, "I can't come home for lunch today because I have to go to the Beatty." This was the company that sold the Beatty washing machines. We didn't have a phone upstairs, and I had run down the stairs to answer the phone. So, he didn't come home, and I accepted that. But this was the kind of thing that used to get to me.

You see, Bill's mother once asked, "Hey Crys, don't you ever tell little white lies?" I guess Bill was brought up with what they called "little white lies."

That evening, when he came home for supper, Bill said to me, "Mom was down to the Hudson's Bay store today"— as if his mother had just spontaneously dropped in. He said she gave him a pair of socks. He showed me the socks, and I said, "Oh, I see."

It was a nice walk from where we lived over to where his folks lived. That evening, we had walked over, and I was visiting with his mother. I think Bill was out in the kitchen getting a snack or somewhere talking to his sisters. It was a "home night," a comfortable, relaxed evening. As I was talking to Bill's mom, I said, "I hear you were downtown today." She said, "Uh, yes, yes." She didn't say anything else, such as what she had done downtown or if she had bought something. There was something off about that conversation. I smelled a rat, and I was hopping mad on our way home.

I gave Bill what for that night. I was very angry. I said, "Not only did you lie, but your mother lied too! You're a couple of liars." I was hot.

I guess Bill thought he'd try to make it right by doing something nice. He didn't. Instead, he brought home a piece of linoleum to cover the floor. Now, in a corner of that front room, there was a slight rise because of the stairway going down. One would have to cut around it to lay the linoleum. He measured it, and I was lying on the chesterfield watching him sweat it out. I didn't care much about the linoleum anyway, and I was still angry. Bill had to turn the linoleum over to cut it. I knew while he was doing it that he was cutting out the wrong corner, but I didn't say a thing. I thought he'd figure it out and fix it. It just didn't matter to me if that thing was put in upside down. That was not my problem. My problem was this business of Bill and his mother lying to me.

So, when Bill turned the linoleum over to place it, he said, "Doggone me. I've cut out the wrong corner."

I didn't say anything. I guess I could be pretty nasty when I couldn't accept some things.

Bill finally got the linoleum in, and it was a nice piece of linoleum, I'll admit. Well, I admitted it years later, but not at that moment. Right then, I didn't care.

Momentous Events

The bombing of Pearl Harbor took place December 7, 1941. We didn't have a television then, just a radio. We heard that San Francisco had imposed a blackout and all the western part of the United States, too. Nobody knew what was going to happen from there. It was a little bit of a shaky thing for all the politicians and the government. I didn't get very uptight about it, but it caused quite a stir. Danny was born on December 10, so that's why I remember it.

Bill visited the hospital. Danny was an angelic-looking baby with perfect features. Bill enjoyed just looking at Danny—a very different experience from when our first baby had been stillborn the year before.

Bill with newborn William Daniel (Danny)

In June 1942, that following year, Bill came home from work quite ill. He went to see Dr. McGrier, who said he was "in a rundown condition." He said that the pain in Bill's head and face that Bill complained about was due to neuralgia. The doctor prescribed medication in pill form and said Bill was to rest. It was like a nervous breakdown from overwork and worry. He took one week of sick leave and two weeks of holiday. Sometime after, Bill began to feel better. We had the house painted ivory with black trim on the windows.

Those are some of the things that happened in those first few years after we married and were living in the little house at 484 Ingersoll Street.

8
The War Years

Bill wasn't present for Danny's second birthday on December 10, 1943. He had received notice from the war office to report for duty at the Fort Osborne Barracks on November 15.[13]

Harold, Marie's husband, worked for the railway. Lloyd, my older brother, worked for the Ford Motor Company in a factory that was turned into an ammunitions factory. Neither Harold nor Lloyd had to leave the country to serve the war effort.

On Saturday, October 30, I had a farewell party for Bill. I didn't like the thought of standing or sitting around and moaning and groaning. I thought the best thing to do was to have a party and have some of his friends over. The party was in my mom and dad's home on Harcourt Street because we were living there at the time. I invited friends from the Hudson's Bay store where Bill worked and some of our close friends as well. It was a group of very different people, twenty-six altogether. Some were very good, and others were peculiar, but then that's the way it was back then.

---

[13] By June 1943, the family had moved back to 202 Harcourt Street, living again with Mom's parents. What led to this move is not known. However, although Mom records that Bill received notice from the war office on November 15, it could be that they were already aware that he would be going at some point and were pro-active in making arrangements.

My friend, Ida, brought some music and played the piano, and everyone sang a bit. Ida's mom had made a fruitcake. Someone who lived next door to my friend Eileen had decorated it in red, white and blue with a "V for Victory" sign and red and blue flowers. On the top in the centre was a little statue I had bought of a man in a soldier's uniform holding a flag. Picardy's Bakery made the sandwiches. We served sherbet glasses filled with jelly and whipped cream, as well as cocoa, Orange Crush and other drinks. We played Bingo and other games and had quizzes. There were prizes such as a wooden cup of shaving soap and men's hankies for the men and three soap elephants and hankies for the ladies.

Lillian and Graham More came. Graham had recently gotten out of the hospital, having just recovered from a ruptured appendix. He brought a record player in a beautifully coloured cabinet and played dance music. It was a lively night, and everyone had a good time. Bill even gave a speech.

I had invited all of Bill's family to come, but none of them came. They were a funny bunch. We did visit his mother or saw her later, but I can't remember how that worked. Later, Bill told me, "Mom said she should have sent Cora." I

Bill's Mom, Bill and Danny

74

answered, "I don't know whether she should have *sent* her, but she should have *let* her come. Cora was a sweet kid, and she would have come to the party if they had let her. I think Cora felt that keenly afterward, but, that's the way they were.

The Single-footer and a Horse Named Billy

My dad had horses then. Bill used to love to ride and did that a fair bit before leaving for the army. Cora came out and spent some time, too. I used to harness up a horse and go for a ride around the hay barn.

We had one horse that my dad called "a single footer" since it moved every foot separately. A special breed, a single footer could go like the wind. It took Bill a little while to realize that once he let that horse get the bit in her mouth, he had to hold on tight! You couldn't control her once that bit was in her mouth. The horse would tear off, and Bill would hang on for dear life. One time, my dad caught him starting to harness that horse up to his buggy. Dad said, "Oh, no! Don't ever put that horse on that buggy! You and the horse and everything will go wild! The buggy will spill over and anybody in it!" So, Bill would just ride her bareback and hang on like glue. She was thrilling to ride. Bill would hang on to the mane or put his arms around her neck. She could rear up, too.

The other horse my dad had was a white horse called Billy, and she was great on the buggy. After Bill had left for the army, there were times when Cora would come, I'd harness up the horse, and we'd go riding around the property. It was fun, and I felt sorry for Cora.

The Last Night

We visited Bill's parents the night before he was to report to the Osborne Barracks. His dad had just gotten over what appeared to be pneumonia. His mother was not too well then, either. I think she had a heart problem. She was going up and down stairs too much to help his dad, and I think that was pretty hard on her. She had just got clear title to her house. She played the horses and had won. Apparently, she had gone down to make the last payment on the house from her winnings when she had suddenly just folded up and collapsed. She never really got over that.

That night, Bill was upstairs in the bedroom to say his goodbyes since his dad was still in bed with pneumonia. His mother said to Bill, "I won't see you again." He said, "Oh, Mom. I'll be back. It won't last that long." She said to him, "Well, you might be back, but I won't be here." She must have known that she wasn't doing well.

Danny was a little duffer then. We came out of the house and got in the car, and Danny was on my knee. Bill's mother then came out of the house saying, "Bill, I forgot about something. I need to see you for a minute."

So, he went back into the house, and I just stayed in the car waiting. When he came back to the car, he looked a little puzzled, and I said, "What was it? What did she want you for?"

The story he told me was that his mother had lost Bill's

Bill's Mom and Bill in uniform,

Danny, 2 years, 7 months

insurance papers. He had two insurance policies. His mother was great for insurance policies on her children, but she was the beneficiary of the one that she continued to carry after he was married. Bill had made me the beneficiary of the other policy. His mom said she had lost the insurance papers and had had them all drawn up again for him to re-sign. He was only in the house long enough for her to explain things and have him sign.

I didn't know that much about insurance policies. My family had never had any. If we had bread and butter at my home, we were happy.

Train Station Goodbye

The time came when Bill had to leave the Osborne Barracks and catch the train to go east. That was a sad time.

The information they were given was very restricted. I don't remember whether he knew what direction he was going, but he phoned me up from the barracks and said they would be pulling out of the CPR station sometime that evening. He didn't know what time. He said, "If I hear any more, I'll give you another call." He did call again and said he only knew they were leaving at six o'clock from the station. Nobody else knew at that moment that he was going that evening except me, so he phoned his mother and told her. I don't know whether Bill was hesitant to get information or whether he couldn't get it. I often wondered. There was so much secrecy about the movement of the army then.

I told Bill I would be down at the station to see him off. He wondered if I could bring a little pair of scissors and a few other things he didn't have. So, I picked up a package of the things he needed and took them to the station.

As I was waiting for the soldiers, I saw them come through the back door, three or four to a row. They marched in like a bunch of puppets, going across the room and up the stairs to where the trains were. As Bill passed, I handed him the parcel, and he took it, afraid to step out of line.

77

Besides me, there was a man and his wife there who had come to see their son off. Of course, some of the men who had signed up to join the army would have come in off the farms, and their folks might not have been able to get down to the station to see them off. But this soldier came down from where the trains were to have a word with his parents. I kept watching and waiting for Bill to come down. I was a little anxious because this wasn't the way to say goodbye, just grab a parcel and keep going.

There was an office off to the side where officials were signing papers. I approached, and a sergeant kindly asked me, "What would you like?" I said, "Well, I've been waiting to see my husband, and he hasn't come down yet. He just went with the others when they marched in. I saw another chap come down to see his parents, and I wanted to know why I couldn't see my husband because I'm here to see him off." He asked, "What's his name?" I told him, and he went up to get Bill.

On each side of the doors, there were guards, corporals. They were standing there as Bill came down through the gate, and one asked him, "What are you doing down here?" Bill said. "I have permission." So, they let him pass.

We hugged and kissed goodbye, and then he had to go, but it gave me the first glimpse of how hard army life was. It was very cruel when you think about it, but that's the way it was.

I hadn't come by car. When I left the station, I hopped on a streetcar and went home to my parents' place on Harcourt Street.

Bill in uniform

Camp Borden and Embarkation Leave

From Winnipeg, Bill was sent to Orillia, Ontario. I don't remember exactly how long he was in Orillia before he was sent to Toronto to take an office training course. From Toronto, he was sent back to Orillia and then to Camp Borden, just west of Barrie, Ontario. When he first went, he was in something called the 2nd Armoured Car Regiment. Then, he was in the infantry. They had to go on ten-mile marches. But, after his office training course, he worked in an office.

He was in an office at Camp Borden for around a year. Occasionally, when he would have a ninety-six-hour leave, he would slip home for a while and then go back.

It was while he worked in the office that Bill asked if he could send for his wife and his son to come for about four months. They said they couldn't guarantee four months, but only two months. Still, it was worth it for me to go down for two months, and I thought it was kind of neat. However, there had been a change in the parliament. James Ralston was the new Defence Minister, and he supported conscription. So, right away, all the men had to go. The government wanted to get the war over with. Danny and I got down to Camp Borden on Armistice Day, November 11,

Bill and Danny   **Bill, Danny and Crystal**

79

1944, and the next day Bill was suddenly given a ninety-six-hour embarkation leave. This was no longer going to be a two-month stay.

During the four-day visit there with Bill, the three of us stayed in a little town nine miles out of Camp Borden full of walnut trees and squirrels. Before Bill had left home for Camp Borden, he had bought a book for Danny called *The Pokey Little Puppy*. Danny had quickly memorized the book, and Bill was amazed that Danny could repeat the story while looking at the pictures.

After those four days, Bill was given three weeks of embarkation leave before he would be sent overseas. So, we went right back home, and during those three weeks, we celebrated Danny's third birthday at Bill's parents' place.

First Signs of a Medical Issue

Bill spent Christmas Day on a ship docked at Liverpool, England. His first rotation when he was stationed over in England was at Aldershot. That was where all the men went at first. I think he was still part of the infantry at that point, even though he had had office training. As I understand it, they went on marches and had to learn to climb over walls and similar things, preparing him to go to France or wherever the heavy fighting was.

They had some leave. On April 9, 1945, according to a letter Bill sent me, he went up to Scotland to visit an aunt of Crosbie, his old friend from high school. He was staying there when he had his first episode of the illness that would affect the rest of his life. He didn't know what it was. All he

Visit in Scotland, 1944

knew was that his coordination was all off and he felt that he should get back to Aldershot. When he got back, he went to the army's Medical Officer. They checked him over and discovered that his reflexes were very poor. They wondered if he'd had a bout of sleeping sickness, encephalitis. He would write and tell me that he was sick but that the doctors couldn't find out his problem. Test results on his chart showed "Nil." The army lowered the category of his physical condition from P1 to P3.[14]

I wasn't there and didn't know how Bill reacted to whatever their findings were. He did tell me one time, "They had me on the train going to the coast to board the ship to France, but they called me off the train." They had given him

---

[14] According to the Physical Standard and Instructions Manual for the Medical Examination of Serving Soldiers and Recruits for the Canadian Army Active & Reserve 1943, P1 meant that the soldier was qualified for full combatant service. P3 allowed duties on lines of communication or at the base.

French money and everything, but they didn't send him. I guess they discovered that he wasn't physically supposed to go at that point. So, he got off the train, and they sent him to Canada House[15] on Trafalgar Square in London.

Trafalgar Square, Canada House marked with an "X"

Dear Dad.

The building in the background is the one where I do my day's toil and tasks.

London is really just another city but so much for that, I thought you might be interested.

Your Son

Bill.

Christmas card sent by Bill to his father in 1945

---

[15] From 1940 to 1947, Canadian Military Headquarters operated out of the Sun Life Assurance of Canada building next door to the Canadian High Commission to the United Kingdom. It was the vanguard for the Department of National Defence in Ottawa, dealing with administrative matters and serving as a command centre for Canadian troops and training. See warmuseum.ca, February 18, 2015.

The Little House on Parkhill Street

I continued sending my letters[16] to Aldershot, but because he had been sent to London, he wasn't getting them. He was writing me and asking what was going on back home. Because he hadn't heard from me, he was getting a little bit anxious about everything. Quite a bit later, he got a whole slew of mail all at one time.

In the meantime, my dad had a little house to sell on Parkhill Street and said I could buy it. I'd written to Bill about it and asked if he would let me know what he thought, but I had to decide on my own. I had to either take it or not take it, and I thought it was a good thing to take it. I went ahead and bought it. I could get it for $1150. That seems an unbelievable amount now, but I only received about $74 a month from the government as Army pay. Then, the government passed a law for something called "family allowance." I filled out the forms that I had received in the mail and got an extra $5 a month for Danny. That little house on Parkhill Street would be what Bill came home to.

Bill, Betty and Big Ben

We had moved back to my mom and dad's place before Bill went into the army. Betty was also living there then.

When Bill was sent to work at Canada House on Trafalgar Square, he had to find a place with board and room because there were no barracks in London. Bill wrote me from London and asked me for our Big Ben alarm clock. It was beautiful and kind of expensive. Betty just had a cheap alarm clock because she had to get up and go to work. I said to Betty, "Look, would you use my clock and then let me send yours? Bill needs to have an alarm because he is

---

[16] Bill's letter to Mom dated April 8, 1945, mentions receiving three letters dated March 22, 26 and 28. Nothing was mentioned about the Parkhill house in his letter. Since the Family Allowance program began in mid-July of 1945, it is assumed that the $5 benefit Mom applied for would have been received in August. Therefore, it is assumed that the purchase and move to Parkhill Street occurred sometime during the summer or fall of 1945.

not living in the barracks, and he needs to get up in time." It wasn't always easy to buy things in those days. There were many restrictions, you had coupons for things, and you could only buy so much. Betty said, "Sure." I thought, "If Bill doesn't bring it back, I guess Betty will have a really nice alarm clock."

Bill's Mother Dies

Bill was still stationed in Trafalgar Square in London, and I was still living at my mom and dad's place on Harcourt Street when Bill's mother died in March of 1945. I had been keeping him posted on his mother because his family had this silly notion, "Don't tell Billy, don't tell Billy." They would never tell Bill how sick she was, but I wrote, "Your mom's pretty sick, and I don't think she is going to be here very much longer." He wrote back and said, "Keep me posted on Mom because they don't tell me anything."

It was around three o'clock that afternoon in March when his mom was rushed to the hospital in terrible pain. Gertie, quite shaken, phoned me to say, "Mom had to go to the hospital." I talked to her a little bit, and she asked, "Do you think we should let Billy know?" I said, "Well, yeah." She asked, "Would you like to let him know?" I said, "Yeah, I can let him know. What will I say? What does the doctor say that her condition is?" She said, "The doctor says she's desperately ill." So, I sent a wire. When Bill got the wire, he wrote me back and said he wanted me to keep him informed. Before I received his reply, his mom had already died, around six o'clock. So, I had to write him again saying that she had passed away.

Gertie Lays Claim

When Bill's mother died, it was discovered that the title of the house was in her name only and not also in her husband's name. The reason, it is assumed, is that his furniture finishing business was located there. If he didn't make it financially with his finishing shop, they didn't want to lose the house. She died without a legal last will and testament. While Bill was overseas, there was some communication by mail between Gertie and him regarding the disposition of the house that was in his mother's name. Gertie had once said, "You know Dad. If he gets into a jam, he'll mortgage our house." I don't know how he could do that because the house wasn't in his name. However, that was one of the reasons Gertie gave Bill to sign over his interest in the house. She said she wanted to take charge and watch over things.

Gertie had written to Bill and told him that she didn't want to do him out of his one-third share in the house but that she needed to have him sign a document so that the house and land would be transferred to her. Bill explained all this to me in a letter he wrote dated April 8, 1945. A lawyer in London had provided Bill with instructions to follow in order to look after his one-third interest. But, against the lawyer's advice, Bill signed the transfer document, sure that everything would eventually work out without any further hard feelings or bitterness. He wanted his dad and sisters to be okay and remain comfortable in their house. Bill had some principles in that regard. With those thoughts in mind, he felt that there really was no alternative but to comply. The lawyer also advised that copies of Gertie's letter to Bill and Bill's reply be sent to me along with a copy of the transfer agreement. He sent them with instructions to keep them safe and never reveal that I had them. If necessary, they could be used as evidence against her if she ever tried to keep their house just for herself.

Bill had advised Gertie that his desire was that his share should be settled in Danny's name. He also suggested she continue to pay the premiums on his life insurance policy that his mom had been paying. In his letter to me, Bill tried to assure me that everything would work out.

9
The Post-War Years

The war was declared over on September 2, 1945. Bill kept working in the office in London until he returned home in April 1946. I was still living with my folks in March 1945, the month that Bill's mom died. Danny and I moved into the house on Parkhill that summer.

Bill and his war medals

When Bill arrived home on April 8, 1946, he was met by a blaze of fire. What a homecoming! The house next door to ours burned down. They carried everything out of the house but the flooring in the kitchen. It had been cemented down. The stove and the heater were all one big unit, and they removed it from the house. I don't know how they ever carried it.

After the house burned down, the owners gave us the first chance to buy the property. They offered to sell it to us for $200. Bill had gratuities from the army that he'd earned overseas, so we used that to buy the property. At the back of that lot, there was a big, very well-built shed. It had not been touched by the fire. We had a seventy-five-foot lot, and that property next door was a seventy-five-foot lot, so we now had a-hundred-and-fifty-foot frontage by about a hundred and thirty feet deep.

Of course, we had an outhouse because there wasn't sewer and water, and we had a well to pump water not too far from our front door. There were beautiful trees on the property, it was a beautiful spot, and we weren't that far off Portage Avenue. That house had been built by the North American Lumber Company when they were making precision houses. It was well put together and well insulated, and it was on a big cement slab—there was no basement.

It was a warm place. The walls did not go all the way up to the ceiling—you could see the two by fours near the top—and that allowed the heat to circulate. But Bill worked to extend those walls up to the ceiling. I was amazed that he could do it, but he did. It was difficult for him to do, but he worked very hard. It was good for his mind, I think, to have something concrete to do. When he was putting on the moulding between the ceiling and the walls, he had a very hard time trying to mitre it. I would stand back and see what was happening, but I couldn't say anything. He worked at that for most of that year, but he got it done.

When Bill came home, one of the first things he bought for the house was a commode. It was a startling green colour. It was placed in the little washroom that had a sink and a basin. We had, of course, to pump and haul our water, which wasn't the most wonderful thing to have to do. Bill, in particular, didn't like living out there with no sewer and no water.

Bill also wanted a car. It was hard to get cars in those days, but he got a Tin Lizzy for a hundred dollars. It was the same colour as our new commode! Bill wanted to drive her all the time, so we often went for a ride. Because he was just a little fellow, Danny sat in front. Bill wanted to be out in that car all the time. He was just like a kid.

Bill was having a rough time adjusting to being home. He didn't want to stay out there on Parkhill Street without running water and flush toilets. It was a beautiful place that we had. I wished he could have been patient for a while longer. I thought it was perfect. But he couldn't grasp those things, and all he wanted at that time was to get a car.

Bill Returns to Work

It was a statutory requirement that when men had to leave their jobs to go to war, they were able to reclaim that same job when they came back. So, that's what Bill ended up doing. He went back to work at the Hudson's Bay Company.

As I recall, there was trouble ever since Bill came home. I used to think he acted strangely at times, and I couldn't figure it out. Different people would say to me, "You have to remember that when a man comes home from overseas, he has a big adjustment to make, taking on responsibilities again which he hasn't had to do when he was in the army." They said that it's quite traumatic for men to come back and face reality again with

Danny, 6 years old, 1947

responsibility for a wife and family. But we only had Danny. I didn't know the nature of Bill's illness. I only knew that they had tested him for what they thought might be sleeping sickness. He did not receive a pension because they said he didn't qualify. Bill just didn't seem to put anything together at home, even with Danny, who was just a little boy. Bill would say, "This kid gets in my hair, you know."

When he was overseas, Bill had gifted me with a washing machine for an anniversary present. I had it at my mom's place. I didn't take it out to the Parkhill home when I moved because that place didn't have running water. My parents had running water even if it was hard water, and I had to get water softener. Still, I took my washing down there because it was too difficult at home. The washing machine was still at my parents' house when Bill came home, and I was still taking my washing down to Mom and Dad's, but Bill had trouble trying to stay and take care of Danny.

Moving to Queen Street

My dad was trying to sell a little house at 279 Queen Street. The owners wanted $3500 for it. We sold ours for $1850, and we made money on that since I had bought it for $1150. So, we had enough for a down payment, and we moved the mortgage over to the new house.

Bill was working at the Hudson's Bay store, and I was trying to pack for the move. It was getting into November, and we were still waiting for the money transactions to go through. There was a large new development called Middlechurch, a neighbourhood of new houses built on one-acre lots. The chap who owned the house on Queen Street had bought one of those houses and had moved in. His mother was taking care of the sale of the Queen Street house. She lived on Parkdale Street and had been going over to the house on Queen Street every day to keep the fires going because it was cold and the house had to be kept warm until we moved in. We didn't have a phone, but she got word to us that she wanted us to move right away. A big snowstorm had begun, and she was becoming quite anxious. It wasn't that easy. Everything was going along okay as far as our lawyer was concerned, so we decided it was okay to go ahead. We were glad to get moved as soon as we could anyway.

We had the movers come out. My knives and forks were still in the drawer, and the table never got packed properly. I had some beautiful silver spoons from my grandma, and I suspect the movers might have helped themselves. Who knows? But we got moved sometime in the middle of that November.

The Hudson's Bay Company used to sell coal for furnaces and mechanical stokers. There was a fellow from the Hudson's Bay Company who installed the stokers, so we got one put in. You would just put a certain amount of coal into a conveyor, like a big arm, and the stoker wound the coal into the furnace. At times we had to blow out "clinkers," the ash and other materials that might not have burned correctly inside the furnace. The stoker was a lot better than having to shovel the coal in all the time.

So, we settled into that house. Our second son, Doug, was born the next April at the Victoria Hospital. Danny started school. We lived at that

Doug and Dan in a haystack at Joseph and Mabel Sloane's place, 1950

place on Queen Street for almost two years.

Berry Street House

By the summer of 1949, the family had moved from Queen Street to 313 Berry Street, on the corner of Ness Avenue and Berry Street. By this time, Danny had been attending school for a couple of years and would be coming up to his eighth birthday. Doug would have had his second birthday the past April. Frank was born in August of 1949 at the - Victoria General Hospital, not long after

313 Berry Street

91

the move. Bill continued to work at the Hudson's Bay store, and Bill's dad was still under contract with the same company, working on the sixth floor refinishing pianos.

Frank, age 6 months, 1950

Faith, 18 months, in a dress made by Crystal, 1954

Phil, age 2, 1959

Faith was born in February 1953. After a miscarriage in June of 1955, Mom became pregnant again, and Phillip joined the family in September of 1956.

Over the years there, several people rented the upstairs suite in our house at different times and for various lengths of time. These included Manuel Parose (who convinced Danny he was a prince of Spain), Elsie McGeehan, Al Winters with his wife and baby, Keith Morrison, and finally Mr. and Mrs. Sinclair and their little girl, Doreen, who lived there in 1959-60. Mr. Sinclair was a photographer. Perhaps as a thank you before they moved out, he took a family picture of us, the only photo ever taken with all of our family members present.

Across from our house, on the corner of Berry Street and Ness Avenue, was Shackell's Grocery, which became Shackell's IGA, owned and managed by Claude Shackell, and the Gifts & Tog Shop, which was managed by his wife Mildred. In the building across the street from Shackell's Grocery on Berry was Gibson's Bakery, and a block down from there was Brathwaite's Drugstore.

Frank, 2, Danny, 10, and Doug, 5, 1959

We lived on Berry Street until January of 1963. What follows occurred on Berry Street.

– Faith Fisher

Bill's Dad Dies

After his wife died in 1945, Bill's father was at a loss, floundering. On October 12, 1950, his father had come down to see Bill at work at the Hudson's Bay store, but Bill had been on a coffee break. When Bill came back, the other fellows told him that his dad had come by to see Bill, but they didn't know where his dad had gone. It was later learned that his dad had collapsed by the elevator on the third floor. He then was taken up to the sixth floor to an infirmary. They called Bill, and he went up. His dad was breathing his last, as Bill put it. Gertie was informed, and she and Cora went down. I was also informed and thought that, I too, should go down.

Bill's dad had just recently bought a new suit on Bill's account at the Hudson's Bay. He would give Bill the money, and Bill would pay on the account. This was just shortly before his father died.

In his father's pocket when he died was a bank book and a twenty-dollar bill. Bill thought he'd give the twenty to Gertie and take the bank book. He had decided that he would see a lawyer and would get things straightened out. So, he kept the bank book. Poor Bill didn't know which way was up. We didn't know who owned the house when his dad died. We had never looked into that as long as his dad was living.

Legal Issues

When Bill went to a lawyer to try to get a settlement, that's when all the skulduggery came out. Bill took everything he had to the lawyer—the letters written by him and Gertie when their mother had died in 1945 and the "Transfer of Rights" document.

Gertie had her own lawyer. Gertie alleged that Bill had signed a Waiver of Claim. She, too, had kept all the letters that he had sent her when he was overseas. In some of her letters, she had underlined particular parts. I don't know what she was trying to prove. Her lawyer had sent photocopies of them to Bill's lawyer. Among all those letters was a Waiver of Claim. Everything had Bill's signature on it except the Waiver of Claim. I guess she threw that in there hoping it would bear some weight, but his signature was not on it.

It became clear Bill would have to take Gertie to court to get his share of the estate. The question was...should he or shouldn't he? He was more stunned over what was happening than anything. He couldn't comprehend Gertie being like this. Gertie stated that the money that her dad had in the bank should go to pay for funeral costs. She was claiming his money and the house—everything. Bill had been back home from the war for four years, and he never recalled having a conversation with Gertie about signing a Waiver of Claim.

Bill had a rough, tough, old lawyer. I was sitting there with Bill, listening. I said something to the lawyer, and he said to me, "It's no business of yours! It is *Bill's* legal problem and *I* am *his* lawyer!" Then he said to Bill, "I'd tell them to go to hell!"

But Bill was not inclined to do that. He would have had to take his sister to court, but he couldn't do it. No settlement was ever reached. Gertie offered to settle for a hundred dollars. That was rejected. Bill didn't want to push it, didn't want to sue his sister in court. So, nothing was ever resolved. That built a wall between Gertie and Bill. Bill didn't get anything at all. He never even got the suit that his father had bought—but Bill had to finish paying for it.

The Emotional Fallout

We never went back to the lawyer again about the issue. About thirty years later, it was discovered that there was a "Settlement Pending" registered on the land title.[17] We never knew.

Bill's family had given him such a hard time when he wanted to get married. I didn't understand it all then, but Gertie had previously turned down a proposal of marriage. So, when Bill wanted to get married, Gertie was dead set against it. His dad just said, "You're a damned fool." His mom said, "You should wait two years." It seemed they all wanted what everybody else had—each other's finances to keep the family going. Bill's dad could do his furniture finishing, his mom could bet on the horses, Gertie could work, and Cora could take care of the home. When Bill decided to marry, it put him in a difficult spot with his family—and yet he loved his family.

When Bill did marry, that gave them more ammunition. They didn't come to the wedding. The struggle with his family continued. Gertie would have nothing to do with the little girl we lost. She wouldn't even go to see her. They didn't see Bill off at the train station when he left for the army. His mom died while he was away. All of those things weighed heavy on Bill's heart.

So, in 1950, after Bill's dad died, there was the furor over the house, there was Gertie's hard attitude, Bill was struggling with adjusting after his return from overseas, and Bill was struggling with his illness. He couldn't put a lot of this together very easily, between his own issues and the animosity that existed. I was wrestling with all of these issues, trying to figure out what was going on. That first Christmas after Bill's dad died, he asked me if I'd invite the girls for Christmas dinner. I phoned them up and invited them. Gertie said that "they had things to do that day" but

---

[17] Gertie outlived her family and remained in the house, alone, until her death. All her assets were converted to cash and dispersed according to her last will and testament, uncontested. Most went to various charities.

would let us know. In other words, she was refusing. When I told Bill, he had that same look that I had seen when our baby girl had died.

10
The Hudson's Bay Company

Meanwhile, life carried on for Bill and me. Bill was working at the Hudson's Bay store. But having that illness seemed to have done something to Bill's head. I was waiting for the "adjustment" that everyone said would take place, but everything seemed to be a big trauma with Bill after that. Then, the trouble at the Hudson's Bay Company began.

After his dad died, Bill had gone over his boss's head to get the job that his dad had had—repairing and refinishing pianos on the sixth floor. His dad had been under contract and not an employee of the company. However, as an employee, Bill was given the opportunity to be in charge of the Piano Repair and Refinishing Shop. He was moved from Appliance and Radios on the fourth floor to a very large area on the sixth floor to work with pianos as his dad had done. He was very happy to carry on this work that he knew and loved to do.

One day in March of 1951, Bill had an episode of illness while working on the pianos. A doctor was called, and Bill told him that it was like one of those spells he'd had overseas. Bill was sent

The Hudson's Bay Company store, 455 Portage Avenue, Winnipeg

home. Right after he'd come home that day, I was trying to fix up the furnace when he had another episode. This was the first time I had ever seen him with amnesia while at home. He didn't know who he was or who we were. I called my brother over. This "spell" went on for about an hour and a half. When Bill came out of it, he just said to get in touch with the doctor at the Hudson's Bay Company, so I called him. When the doctor came to the phone, he asked if Bill could talk with him, and I said, "Just a minute." Turning towards him, I said, "Bill, the doctor wants to talk with you." So, Bill talked with him. I then had to phone the drugstore to send out some pills the doctor had prescribed. The pharmacist sent them over, but before they arrived, Bill seemed to get overheated in the head. He ended up in the hospital for three weeks.

Because Bill connected this spell with what he'd had overseas, I went down to the Department of Veterans' Affairs. I told the doctor there exactly what had happened, and he wrote everything down.

Bill had his holidays coming up in June, and it seemed like a good idea for him to go on a trip. He hopped on the bus and went down east. His mother had relatives there and some in Detroit.[18] He visited with some of them and then went up to Windsor and visited with some of my relatives. He was away for about ten days. He had a great trip and felt much better.

But when Bill returned to work, he found that the Piano Shop that he had worked so hard at had been destroyed. The tools and equipment were spread from one end of the sixth floor to the other, and there was a stack of merchandise in place that had not been there before. They had never said a thing to Bill about what they were doing. He went down to the fourth floor and asked what was going on. The boss was away on his holidays, and nobody knew anything.

---

[18] Bill sent a telegram to Gertie from the Barlum Hotel in Detroit on August 20, 1948, stating, "Sent special air mail today. All is well." Bill was then thirty-three years old.

The Spark

The old boss didn't return, and now Bill had a new boss. Bill wasn't used to him, and he was never very happy after that.

The story I was told went like this: The fellow who had installed the stoker at our place on Queen Street would be called to remedy a problem with a stoker that had previously been installed. He would go out to the home and take care of whatever the problem was. The customer would pay cash for the repair, and the fellow would bring the money to the store. But, apparently, this fellow wasn't turning in the money. How he

could get away with that, I don't know.

One time when the Hudson's Bay Company's management took stock in that department, they found they were about $1800 short. If a repairman would go out to fix something, he would take some parts from stock in order to do the repair. He would charge the people, but he either didn't record taking the stock or he didn't turn the money in.

The company brought someone in to clear up the problem. As I understood it, Bill was "called up on the carpet"—questioned about what was going on with the stock.

There was a

Passing Show

The Passing Parade takes you to the Third Floor, to hear the latest news.

Dept. 110 - MILLINERY
Goodbye was said to MISS M. CHERRY, who is now to be found in the Dress Accessories, and a big Hello to KAY SUL, our new co-worker.

Dept. 102 & 103 - WOMEN'S SUITS AND COATS
Welcome to MRS. L. FAIRBAIRN a new member of the staff. It's nice to have DOUG REEVES back at work, after a short trip to the hospital.

Dept. 112 - SPORTSWEAR
The gang all spent a very enjoyable afternoon out at Tyndall, at the summer home of MRS. DOROTHY OLIVER. Mr. Oliver showed everyone the district sight, the Tyndall Quarries.
We are very sorry to announce that our amiable DON DAMPSY is leaving the store to spend a short while in England.

Dept. 120 & 120T - MADEMOISELLE SHOP - TEENER SHOP
MR. A. COOK is the new face in our department. He has been looking after things while MR. LEFEBVRE is on a Buying Trip.

Dept. 126 - LINGERIE
Welcome to MR. JACK PLAICE, hope you like working in the woman's world.

Dept. 606 - BEAUTY SALON
Congratulations to MR. & MRS. JAMES TOAL (RUTH) on the arrival of their new baby daughter LONNIE RUTH, on June 13.

Dept. 54-01 - 3 FLOOR MARKING ROOM
Welcome to ART GRIFFITH who has been transferred from the 6th floor
We all miss MR. JACK BRADY who has now retired. Many pleasant years ahead for you JACK.

Long Service News

GUESS WHAT!

The Beaver Magazines are now in and can be obtained at the Personnel Office.

- - - -

It's all right to soak up facts like a blotter but remember that a blotter gets everything backwards.

- - - -

Have you moved recently? If so, have you given your change of address and phone number to the Staff Records?

- - - -

Please remember that it is important that you do this.

- - - -

Moment's silence in theatre after movie hero slaps villainess and strides off. Child's voice, "Mama, why didn't she hit him back like you always do?"

Women's Tears - the first successful Fluid Drive.

- - - -

GIRLS - Those sheer nylon blouses are very pretty - but NOT for business. Please do not wear them to work.

Congratulations to the following members of the Staff who have received Long Service Awards this month -

25 years
Mr. W. Morris, Men's Cloth, Basement.

15 years
Mr. W. Baluk, Bake Shop.

10 years
Miss D. Bywater, Sportswear
Mrs. M. Tye, China
Miss J. Young, Restaurant
Mrs. F. Lowry, Drapery Workroom.

- - - -

GOLFERS......
Watch that notice board outside the Staff Lunch Room! Have you played your game off yet? If not please get it off quickly as we want to be sure and get all the games played off by early in Sept. Also watch for the notice on the Ladies' and Men's Field Days and Mixed Two-Ball Foursome that will be coming up early in September.

FORE!!

co-worker who worked across the hall from Bill who fixed washing machines. Bill told me that the two of them had a feeling about what the stoker repairman was doing, and they attempted to figure out what was going on. When they had some evidence, Bill took it to his boss, who told him to "take it up to the fifth floor." Bill didn't want to do that. He had got the information for the boss, and he thought the boss should take it up. But the boss said he had no alternative, so Bill took it up. They called the stoker fellow in and questioned him and found out that what Bill had discovered was true. The fellow wasn't charged. His employment was just terminated. Mr. Warrington, who Bill reported to on the fifth floor, paid him fifteen dollars for his work in uncovering the thefts, and the other worker received ten dollars. At least, that's what Bill told me.

The Flame

According to Bill, after they had got that stoker business resolved, there seemed to be other things that the managers wanted Bill to look out for. Bill could see other things going on and not just with the ordinary workers but also with the higher-ups. He would get annoyed at how some of these higher-ups did things. He said sometimes they'd have merchandise sent out to their cabins. Bill said he would complain about this to whomever he could. There was a man named Abramson[19]—I think he was the manager of the Hudson Bay store—and there was Bill's boss, Mr. Warrington.[20] There was also a "store representative," Glen Lucas, who I think was essentially a store detective. Bill talked a lot about the "big shots" who would steal things. He told me that he began to "stooge" around Lucas. They wanted Bill to find out more about what Lucas was saying

---

[19] According to the June 1952 edition of *The Bayville News*, the Hudson's Bay Company's staff publication, Mr. N.H. Abramson began his duties as Store Manager that month.
[20] Albert E. S. Warrington was employed by the Hudson's Bay Company from 1915 to 1954 and received two long-service awards.

about these other big guys. So, Bill started to become acquainted with the guys who were doing things and taking things.

It got to the point where Bill got mixed up with these men. It seemed that most of the planning and transactions were done in the beer hall, and Bill would be there. Bill told me they would have him set up something, supposedly in order to catch the thieves. He would get everything all set up, and then he would go to these higher-ups and tell them that it was okay—they could go and do what they needed to do. But then they would come up with some technical reason why they couldn't do it that particular night. Bill had set it all up for nothing. One time, Bill told me they had him plant marked merchandise in different places so that when these men took something that was marked, they could be caught.

I also remember Bill telling me that this thing had grown bigger than he ever thought it would. It scared him because there was a ring of thieves in the city who were also stealing things from other businesses. It seemed he had gotten himself into an awful stew toward the end of it all. It is possible that the people who were benefitting from this thievery were the same ones who were having Bill do the marking so that they knew what was going on and who was going to blow the whistle.

What Could I Do?

It took me quite a while to find out what was really going on. Bill was coming home late and often looking like he was in a state of shock. As he got in deeper and deeper, he got more shook up. He had it all built up in his mind that he was going to get about $5,000 if he helped catch the thieves, which was a tremendous amount of money. I could never fathom the whole thing. I remember saying, "Bill, I wouldn't do that for the king of England. You don't have a leg to stand on! You're doing this?! You're as guilty as the next guy!" And he was, because they had involved him in the transactions themselves.

I began to realize what was going on, and I didn't like it. I said to him, "Bill, I have to think of the family. I have to go to a lawyer for the protection of the family."

And he said, "Don't you dare interfere!"

What could I do? My husband was saying, "Don't you dare interfere. I know what I'm doing." He thought he knew what he was doing when it started out. He thought he was doing a wonderful thing for the company.

The Fire

Bill didn't think I believed him, things were getting more intense, and he was getting more uptight. One time, he phoned me and said, "Crystal, I want you to take a cab and come down to 202 Maryland Street." That was south of Portage. I was afraid to go alone because I had heard so many crazy things. I was afraid they would get me down there and hold me hostage or something. So, I phoned my dad and told him what was going on. He was in his 70s, not young, but he came and drove me to Maryland Street. I said to him, "Dad, I'll go in, but, if I'm not back out here in five minutes, I want you to come in." He said, "Okay."

202 Maryland Street, 2022

So, I went into this detective's home. They started to talk a little bit about what Bill was doing. The detective was trying to convince me that they couldn't do this without Bill. "But," he said, "we have to be very careful because if they find out what we're doing and what your husband is doing, he can serve as much as two years for a felony."

Now, I didn't know what a felony was, and I couldn't understand why a place like the Hudson's Bay Company would involve Bill in something where he could be accused of a felony. But that's what the detective told me, and Bill was there. I was not convinced. But Bill was sure everything was good, and he wanted me to understand what was going on.

I said, "Look, my dad is out in the car, and I told him I'd go out and bring him in." So, I went out and brought him in. Dad sat in a chair and listened to everything they were saying. They repeated that they couldn't do this job without Bill and all the rest of it. My dad sat there and listened. After it was all finished, Dad drove Bill and me home. I was left with a conundrum. I looked up what a felony was in the dictionary. I still could not grasp it—Bill had received the first money from Mr. Warrington, who was now offering Bill $5000? I think they must have all been involved—Abramson, Warrington and the detective Lucas.

Silence and Blackmail

Percy White was the personnel superintendent of the store. Evangeline Shogren, who was the daughter of the pastor at Grant Memorial Baptist Church where we had been attending, worked for him. I was pretty sure she knew what was going on. She couldn't do anything about it, and I was advised by somebody not to involve her. She wouldn't be able to tell me what was going on because she was sworn to secrecy working for Percy White in the personnel department.

Bill eventually told them that he didn't want to do this work anymore, but they said that they would just finish this one job. So, he agreed to finish that one job. They seemed to keep leading him along with the suggestion that he would be getting quite a large sum of money. So, Bill was still carrying on. I was told that they had caught a lot of those who were involved in the thefts and they had been fired.

One day, a letter came into our mailbox addressed to Bill. I figured it was about time I knew a few things, so I opened it. The writer stated that he had overheard Bill talking with the other fellows and he knew what Bill was up to. He said that if Bill didn't pay him a certain amount of money, he was going to report Bill. It was blackmail. I gave that letter to Bill and said to him, "Bill, I don't know what your trouble is, but you had better confess to whatever is going on and clear the air."

Bill Is Arrested

The stores used to close at one o'clock in the afternoon on Wednesdays. That had started sometime during the war years and was still in effect. On a Wednesday not long after our discussion about confessing, Bill phoned me and said he had to work late and wouldn't be home until suppertime. But he didn't come home for supper. At about a quarter to eight, I had a phone call from the police saying that my husband wanted to see me. I said, "Well, I'm here. He can come and see me." The caller said, "If you want to see him, you have to come down to the police station." I figured things were coming to a climax.

At that time, Al Winter and his wife and baby were living upstairs. They had gone down to King's Theatre on the corner at Portage Avenue to a particular event held on Wednesday nights, and they had asked me to watch the baby. I phoned the theatre and asked if they would find the Winters and give them a message to call me, which they did. Al and his wife knew a little bit about what was going on. I used to be up washing and waxing the floors at midnight and early in the morning to pass the time. They knew it was something to do with Bill and the Hudson's Bay Company. On the phone, I told Al that I had to go to the police station and see Bill, and Al said they would leave right away and walk home.

I called a taxi to go down to the police station, leaving my kids and their little baby at home. As the taxi was pulling away from the house, I asked the taxi driver to stop for a minute so I could talk to the couple we could see coming down the street. He stopped, and I told Al that I was going now. He asked me if I wanted him to come. I said that would be great. So, his wife, Eileen, continued on home, and Al came with me in the cab to the police station.

By the time I got down there, it was getting quite late, almost a quarter to nine. I went up to the wicket, gave my name to the officer standing behind it and said that I'd come to see my husband.

He shouted, "We don't let anybody in here after eight o'clock!"

St. James police station and fire hall. The police station had 30 steel cells.

I said, "I don't care what *you* do. You didn't phone me till just before eight, I'm here, and I want to see my husband!" I was angry.

He said, "We'll give you ten minutes."

There was a detective standing beside me for all of those ten minutes. There was a big cage. When Bill came out, the first thing that I asked him was, "Bill, did you do anything wrong?"

He said, "Yes."

I said, "Okay."

He couldn't tell me everything right then, but I knew what had gone on.

He said, "I have to be on the docket at ten o'clock in the morning."

I didn't know exactly what that meant, but I knew that it was a terrible situation. I said, "Okay," and returned home.

The Queen vs William Francis Hay

As soon as I got home, I phoned the lawyer that we had had for the business with Gertie: Hart Green. I phoned him at home and told him who I was. I said, "I have to see you first thing in the morning."

He asked, "Would ten o'clock be alright?

I said, "No, it won't."

He said, "9:30?"

"Yeah," I said. "I'll be there at 9:30."

When we met, I started telling him what the Hudson's Bay Company had done, having my husband arrested. I was trying to give him the story, but he immediately picked up the phone and arranged to have Bill remanded for a week before he got up on the docket. I didn't even know what "up on the docket" meant.

Then I told Mr. Green all that I could tell him. He said, "Okay. I'll contact you to come again." He went down to talk with Bill. Following his talk with Bill, Mr. Green contacted me again. He said, "I'm afraid he's in the soup."

It seems that when Bill had phoned me up at noon on that Wednesday and said he had to work late, he had apparently been "called up on the carpet." He wrote everything out while he was at the store, confessing. He had been angry because I had told him, "Bill, whatever's going on, you had better confess it and get rid of it because it's driving you crazy and it's going to ruin you and the whole family." That's what they nailed him on. The first thing Hart Green had said to Bill was, "Never write out a confession."

I never saw the confession that Bill wrote. The next time I saw Hart Green, he said, "It doesn't make for good reading." He advised me not to read it, so I didn't. It wouldn't have done me any good. Whether Bill was angry when he wrote it or whatever else was in his mind, I don't know.

Arranging Bail

Bill could be released on bail, but I needed to have two different people who would help. They didn't have to give the cash. They only had to have a thousand dollars each that they could get if necessary. One was Bill Funk, and the other was one of the couples at the church[21] at that time, Mr. and Mrs. Magnusson. However, when Bill Funk went down to secure the money, it was discovered that he did not own the house that he lived in! He had not known that his name was not on the title. He had bought this house, but it was his lawyer's name that was on the title, not his. So, he wouldn't be able to help. It threw him into a tizzy when he found that out. He had to get it straightened out because he was making mortgage payments on a house he didn't own.

So, Charlie and Ann West[22] and Mr. and Mrs. Herman Magnusson helped to arrange bail for a thousand dollars each because they owned property. Bill was finally released on bail.

A small article appeared in the *Winnipeg Tribune* that May, stating that Bill had been charged with theft and had been released on bail. From the notoriety, you'd think that Bill was a murderer. But it was the big Hudson's Bay Company against Bill.

After he got out on bail, Bill got a job with another furniture finisher. The man that he worked for was quite a drinker. Bill worked in a basement somewhere, not too far from Toronto Street where his sisters lived.

---

[21] By 1950, Bill and Mom, as well as her parents, were attending Grant Memorial Baptist Church on Colony Street. It is believed that all of the people posting bail were attending the church at that time. These names were known to us in relationship to the church. At this time, the archival material for the church has not been organized and is in storage, not available for viewing.

[22] Ann West was a half sister to Hilda Bystrom, another good friend at the church.

Bill said one time that he'd come home and paint our kitchen. We needed to have the kitchen painted, so I got busy and scrubbed all the kitchen walls so that when he came home, they'd be all clean for him to paint. But he didn't come home as he had said he would. That was the beginning of a lot of bad things.

Bill was still out on bail when he was called to appear in September for what was called the Fall Assizes. At the Assizes, his date for a court hearing was set for December 17, 1952. I guess his nerves were shot. He ended up in the hospital that day with a terrible case of diarrhea.

In the meantime, I was running up a little bit of a grocery bill at Shackell's grocery store across the street from us on Ness Avenue. Mr. Shackell knew that there was a problem, but he didn't know the full extent of it.

The Sentencing Hearing

On December 17, 1952, we went down for a hearing to be held that afternoon. Pastor and Mrs. Shogren from the church were there, and my dad was with me. I didn't know much about lawyers or legal proceedings because I had never had much to do with them, but I remember a lawyer telling me to look sad. I didn't have the heart to do it. I don't know what he was trying to do.

This was not the trial.[23] One of the things I remember the prosecutor saying was that this was not an isolated incident, but he didn't say what any other incidents could have been. Nothing was said at this hearing about the store

---

[23] A preliminary hearing had been held on October 2, 1952. Mom was not in attendance. The prosecutor was Mr. Tupper, and Mr. Green acted as the defence counsel. Glen Lucas appeared on behalf of the Hudson's Bay Company, and witnesses were called to give their accounts. The case was committed for trial. A "speedy trial" occurred at 10:30 in the morning of the same day as the sentencing hearing. Mom seemed unaware of this.

detective Lucas, who I understood had engaged Bill on behalf of the company. According to Bill's lawyer, Bill had confessed in writing, and so he was guilty as charged.

The sentencing hearing that afternoon wasn't very long. The judge sentenced Bill to a year. I ran down to hug Bill and said, "This is so unfair!" I thought I knew what was going on. It seemed to me to be so unfair, that nothing could be done against a big company like the Hudson's Bay. So, they took Bill away. An article appeared in the *Winnipeg Tribune* on Wednesday, December 17, saying that Bill had been found guilty of theft and sentenced.

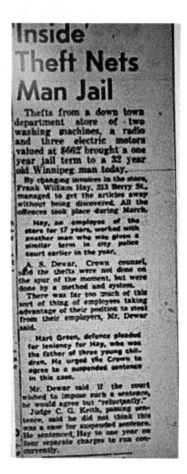

'Inside'
Theft Nets
Man Jail

Thefts from a down town department store of two washing machines, a radio and three electric motors valued at $662 brought a one year jail term to a 32 year old Winnipeg man today.

By changing invoices in the store, Frank William Hay, 213 Berry St., managed to get the articles away without being discovered. All the offences took place during March.

Hay, an employee of the store for 17 years, worked with another man who was given a similar term in city police court earlier in the year.

A. S. Dewar, Crown counsel, said the thefts were not done on the spur of the moment, but were done by a method and system.

There was far too much of this sort of thing of employees taking advantage of their position to steal from their employers, Mr. Dewar said.

Hart Green, defence pleaded for leniency for Hay, who was the father of three young children. He urged the Crown to agree to a suspended sentence in this case.

Mr. Dewar said if the court wished to impose such a sentence, he would agree but "reluctantly."

Judge C. G. Keith, passing sentence, said he did not think this was a case for suspended sentence. He sentenced Hay to one year on four separate charges to run concurrently.

11
Picking Up the Pieces

Earlier that year, I had had a thyroid operation, which had upset my cycle, and I had become pregnant. When Bill

was sentenced, I was seven months' pregnant. After we left the courthouse, my dad and I were going home. However, I knew I was going to need welfare, and I knew I already owed Shackell's Grocery[24] seventy-five dollars for groceries. So, I asked my dad to take me to Shackell's. We had been buying from there for quite a while. I told Mr.

Mildred and Claude Shackell

Shackell what had just happened, and he said to me, "Now you keep on buying groceries here just like you've been doing." I could have cried. They were very good to us.

From there, Dad took me down to the

Shackell's Grocery Store, circa 1932

---

[24] Claude and Mildred Shackell operated the grocery store (eventually Shackell's IGA) and a dry goods store (Gifts & Tog Shop) in St. James for forty years.

municipal hall to apply for welfare. I spoke to a man there named Mr. Brown, told him what had happened, and said that I needed welfare. He was so gentle, kind and understanding. There was no problem. They didn't pay cash, but they gave out vouchers. They had the vouchers made out for Shackell's Grocery, but only thirteen dollars a week. Welfare paid directly for things such as the mortgage and electricity.

Setting Up the Meeting with Abramson

After I came home, Pastor Shogren and his wife came over. I could tell him a bit more now because previously I couldn't involve his daughter Evangeline, who worked with Percy White in the personnel department at the Hudson's Bay Company. I didn't want to say too much. I said what I could, but I felt finished, tired of talking.

He asked, "Would you like to see Mr. Abramson?"

I said, "Yes, I would be very glad to do that because I had never had a chance to talk to him. I didn't know I could."

Pastor Shogren said that he would go and see him. Mr. Abramson phoned me up the very next day, right after Pastor Shogren had seen him. He said, "I understand you'd like to talk with me?" When I said yes, he agreed to meet with me "as soon as the holidays are over." So, we made an appointment for January 3rd or 5th.

The next day, Friday, I was still having a lot of trouble physically and was in a lot of pain. Betty came over and phoned Dr. Jack Brenner, who had taken over obstetrics from Dr. McGrier. When I talked with him, I said something about not having any money. He answered, "Money is only paper. You just get hold of yourself." He also said he knew the lawyer, Hart Green. Apparently, Mr. Green had threatened the Hudson's Bay Company, saying that they had better be lenient with Bill or he would expose them with bad publicity. Bill had been sentenced to a year, but I didn't know then that the company had wanted him sentenced to five years. I thanked Dr. Brenner. He told me to take a 222 or something, but it didn't help.

First Visit to Headingley Jail

One o'clock on Tuesdays was visiting time at the Headingley Jail. I made up my mind I was going to be there right at one o'clock, no matter what. It was arranged that my mom and dad would come down and stay with the kids.

In the morning while I was preparing to leave, there was a knock at the back door. I was trying to get lunch and feed the kids and my mom and dad. When I opened the door, there was the Hudson's Bay Company driver. He said, "Mrs. Hay, we have some parcels for you. I said, "Just put them on my kitchen floor."

I thought that maybe the church had sent out a hamper, so I didn't pay much attention. But he kept putting parcels on the floor and going out and coming back in with more parcels and going out and coming back. When he was through, I couldn't walk across my kitchen floor. Then I had to sign a paper saying that I had received these groceries. On the paper, I could see that the person who had sent these groceries out was Percy White, and I thought, "What is that company doing?!" I was feeling very angry that they would do that, but at that moment I didn't have any time to figure things out. I signed the paper and let him go.

I was so angry to think that that store would do one thing (send Bill to jail) and then do that (give me groceries). But I had no choice at the time but to get the groceries out of the way because I had to get going. I cleaned off some shelves and started stacking the food there. Then I noticed that there was everything. They hadn't just sent out tins of peas, but they had sent "sieved peas"—in large, twenty-eight-ounce cans. They hadn't just sent out asparagus, but asparagus spears. There were more tins than I could count. They had sent four tins of honey and four tins of jam. And a turkey! The dressing was sent out separately, and cranberries and cranberry sauce and gravy. There were sausages and all kinds of things. I couldn't believe it. Going by prices then, there must have been about two hundred dollars worth of groceries. I realized that I would be able to pay Shackell's off, and then all I would have to buy was bread and milk. At the end of each month, I had only about three dollars left, but with that I could buy the kids ice cream cones!

My dad drove me out to Headingley, but I visited Bill by myself. I was seven months pregnant. Bill and I talked about the baby that was coming, and he said that if it was a girl, he would name her Faith Crystal—"That's what we'll call her." That's the name she got.

While I was away that afternoon visiting Bill, the phone rang at home, and, although my mom was around, Danny answered it. They asked him how we got our heat. Did we have to put coal in the furnace? Did we have to turn a thermostat? Danny told the caller that we shovelled it into the furnace. So, the caller knew that we used coal. The next day, about a ton of coal was delivered.

On another day, the telephone rang again, and Betty took the call. The caller said, "We'd like to know the ages of the boys that live there." Betty asked, "Who's calling?" The caller said, "It's Santa Claus, and I just need the ages of the boys." Danny was eleven, Doug was four or five, and Frank was two or three. The caller had said he was Santa Claus, and that was all we knew.

The Real Santa Claus

In the Hudson's Bay store, there was a beautiful rest room. It was a place where you could bring your babies and leave them with staff while you shopped—which I used to do with Doug when he was a baby. I got to know the woman who worked there. She was a very lovely Christian woman, and she kept a good eye on things while the mothers shopped. After those groceries were delivered, as soon as I had a chance to go up to the store, I talked with her. I told her what had happened, and she said, "It wasn't the store that did that. It was all the employees in the store who knew your husband.

I cried. I had had to sign so that Percy White would know that I had received them. Now I knew that it wasn't the company that had sent them. It was the people. The next time I went down to see Bill, I told him about it.

I was able to visit Bill one or two more times again before the baby was born. The doctor had told me that when she was born, he would phone out to Headingley to let Bill know. She was born February 19, 1953.

Letters and Visits with Bill

Pastor Shogren from Grant Memorial Baptist Church also went to see Bill once or twice. Then there was a lot of trouble at the church, and there was a split. Pastor Shogren was to leave at the end of December, but, before he left, another man was appointed to visit Bill. He worked at Eaton's. It was arranged with the jail that he could visit Bill.

Different people wrote letters to Bill while he was there. A couple who lived over on Guilford Street wrote Bill a letter. So did Betty's husband, Walter.

I used to write him letters, too. I especially remember one of them. It was when spring[25] had come and the snow had gone and the leaves were coming out on the trees. I wrote about how life had sprung up after the dead of winter and said it was another sign of life after death. I wrote a little bit more along that line. All letters were censored at the jail. Bill told me much later that the sergeant had called him in to get his letter. Of course, they had read it in order to censor it, and he said to Bill, "We don't receive many letters like this here." I guess it was something that spoke to the powers that be in there too. I don't know.

---

[25] Bill's birthday was in the spring, May 27.

Sometime after Faith was born, I took her out for Bill to see her. Then, a few weeks later, I took her out again. But I began feeling unwell. I would get those spells of feeling unwell off and on. I think it was all nerves. I didn't seem to be able to control a lot of things. The second time I took her out must have been in April, about six weeks after she was born. Around this time, some people had begun writing letters in support of Bill's parole.

Meeting at The Bay

On Monday, January 5, 1953, I think—I'm not sure exactly, but it was shortly after New Year's Day—I went up to talk to Mr. Abramson at about 2:00 in the afternoon.

This was the situation. After they had caught the other fellows that Bill had helped them catch, they let them all out—they were never charged. Also by now, other employees had left the Hudson's Bay Company. There was a fellow who worked as a floor manager whose last name was Gandy. He had become friends with Bill, and we used to visit with him and his wife in their home. But Mr. Gandy had left the company. The store detective, Lucas, had gone—he had just sort of walked off the face of the earth with no accountability for involving Bill. And Mr. Warrington had left. I heard that he went to work for Investors Syndicate.

So, at this meeting, Mr. Abramson had brought with him the man who had taken Mr. Warrington's place, Mr. Tingley. He was new on the job. I think Mr. Tingley was brought in to this meeting for Mr. Abramson's benefit.

One of the questions that I asked Mr. Abramson was, "How come those people that Bill helped you get, you let them all out, but when it come to my husband, you had him sentenced?"

I wondered why Mr. Tingley was there. So, I said to him, "You must have thought from the files that my husband was the culprit."

He said, "What files?"

116

I said, "You mean to tell me that you're working here and you know all about this, but you've never seen the files or any other records that were kept about what was going on?"

I think he didn't want to admit it. He said, "The worse thing that your husband did was to involve another man."

I said, "Well, I understand that other man was already going by an alias. He apparently had done a term in jail before. Knowing that that man had served a term before, that he knew what he was doing, I can't buy the idea that my husband involved him." Tingley made me angry because he'd never been there before, but he was trying to make out that Bill was worse than he was. I remembered Bill telling me about this man who was using an alias. I often wondered why they had put that man there to work alongside Bill anyway.

Abramson said to me, "Your husband could have told us much more than he did."

I said, "I'm sorry he told you anything to start with."

He said, "We have a policy in our store that if someone is doing something wrong, whatever they were caught doing should be reported. If they are not reported, then those who knew and were protecting them are also guilty. They are accomplices."

I said, "Look, I have three boys. I never teach my boys to squeal on each other. I don't think that's a good policy that you have." I was very emphatic about that point.

I was up there for a good couple of hours. Near the end, he said that if they could do anything for me, I should let them know.

I said, "Well, if you can take the ironer back to pay off what we owe, I would appreciate that."

Bill had bought me an electric mangle thing to do ironing with. It was a big thing with a big arm. I'd sit down and do all the ironing with it. We hadn't had it very long, but it had been fully paid for. We were making payments on a piano, and we might have owed for some coal and maybe

117

even the suit that his dad had bought before he died. I think there were also some other little things that we had needed and had bought. So, Abramson agreed to do that. They took the ironer back, and that was a good thing because it cleared off whatever debt Bill had owed.

Out on Parole

I hadn't gotten out to visit Bill after that time I had seen him in April and was feeling unwell. Bill became eligible for parole, and he was released in the summer of 1953. He had only served seven months. He wasn't released to go home immediately. He had to spend some time at a place downtown.[26] He could wash cars that belonged to those who worked there and things of that nature. I don't know whether he made a little money doing it or not, but at least he was not behind bars.

August 1954, following Bill's release from prison

Bill, Gertie and Cora

Bill, Faith, 6 months, and Cora

Alpha Furniture Finishers

After Bill came home, he went back to work for the finishing company he had worked at before starting his sentence. He worked there for a while, but the owner was a heavy drinker and ended up in the hospital with tremors trying to go cold turkey to get off the booze.

---

[26] That is, a halfway house.

It was decided that Bill should establish his own business.[27] At the time, a young lawyer named Keith Morrison[28] and his wife were living upstairs in our house. He had a small office on Portage Avenue, and he was able to help us get the business started—Alpha Furniture Finishers. We arranged to increase the mortgage on our house enough so that Bill could start up his business. We put the house in my name, which would eventually prove to be a good thing.

Danny, 13, Frank, 7, and Doug, 5, August 1954

Kitty-corner from our house on Berry Street and Ness Avenue was a bakery,[29] and behind it was a red building. We were able to rent it from the owners for Bill's shop. When he had that little shop out behind the bakery, I was amazed at the amount of work that he put through. He had that shop all winter, and then in the spring the owners said he couldn't continue there because it was not a suitable place for his business.

Bill needed to get a more proper set-up. That's when he rented a shop on Madison Street. I don't know what it was, but he was not as settled there as he was when he had been behind the bake shop. I was doing the bookkeeping for him, and he worried me because he couldn't seem to settle into the work there. It was a bigger shop, with higher overhead, and therefore he needed to have more work run through to keep the overhead paid and bring money home. It was his own business, there were a lot of responsibilities, and I think he was trying to get help. The fire inspectors would

---

[27] This would have been in the spring of 1954.

[28] This was not the celebrity with the same name who was in the news all the time then.

[29] Gibson's Bakery.

come around sometimes and say things such as, "You can't spray anymore until this and this are done." Those things would trouble him. He didn't know how to solve problems that wouldn't be that difficult for an ordinary person. It was too difficult for him to make decisions. He used to say to me, "Oh, I wish I had a job where I just punched holes in doughnuts." The Madison Street location was not a good place for him.

The Berry Street Shop

We heard of a building that was for sale, but it had to be moved. A big cement slab was poured in the space behind our house, and we got the building moved. Bill was delighted about that. We had lots of things done, even in the house. We had still been dragging coal ash from the house out to the garbage at the back, but somehow we were able to get a gas furnace. Bill worked better in the new space, but he still had some terrible spells, and we still didn't know what his problem was. Phillip was born that September.

**The concrete foundation being poured for
Bill's furniture refinishing shop**

12
The Final Years:
A Stormy Period

(Note: The following events took place during the years of 1957-1962. The order in which they took place is not always clear.)

The years from 1954 to 1962 were years of trouble. After Bill came back from incarceration, his spells became more frequent and more violent. The police had to come to the house several times and take him to the Deer Lodge

Family photo 1958
Back: Frank, Dan, Doug
Front: Bill, Faith, Phil, Crystal

Hospital because it seemed he was going mad. One time when I had to call the police, Bill yanked the phone receiver from my hand and pulled the cord out. It was going from bad to worse. Bill had spells of amnesia, severe head pain, catatonic behaviour and even erratic behaviour. Sometimes, he violently attacked furniture and fixtures. One time, the breaking up of furniture could be heard across the street inside Shackell's Grocery Store. It sounded like breaking glass. There was never any violence against the children or me. He never laid a hand on people. He was in and out of Deer Lodge Hospital[30] several times during these years, all while the children were growing up.

For a period of time, Bill displayed what I would describe as over-exuberant behaviour because of prescription drugs I discovered he was taking. About three to four days a month, I would have a terrible headache. I thought the top of my head was going to blow off. I went to see a Dr. Anderson in the Winnipeg Clinic, and he prescribed some pills. They were Benzedrine, mood elevators. I was to take them about three to four days before I would get these headaches, and everything would be fine after that. That's the only time that I took them, for four days each month. Without my knowledge, Bill tried them. They made him feel like he was on cloud nine, and I couldn't figure out why. For a while he would be on cloud nine, what happened in the shop didn't bother him one iota, everything was looking rosy, and his mind was released of tension—but that was all. Everything else would go to pot.

During the summer, Douglas delivered newspapers. One Saturday, I had taken the three younger children, Frank, Faith and Phillip to the Sunday school picnic at the park. Bill, of course, would be working in his shop.

---

[30] It was during this very stormy period that the "Kobrinsky Boat" came along and the actions of its "captain" eventually provided us with an "anchor." For a time, Dr. S. Kobrinsky worked at the Deer Lodge Hospital with war veterans. It is believed this was where he met Bill.

When I came home from the picnic, I asked Doug, "How'd you make out?"

He said, "Oh, fine. I went to the drugstore and got Dad some pills.

I repeated, "You went to the drugstore and got Dad some pills?"

"Yeah", he said, "I've been there before and got them for Dad."

I said, "You have!?"

I was the only one allowed to get this prescription filled. I went over to Braithwaite's Drugstore to inquire as to how Bill could get the pills.

Around this time, there was a new druggist. He said to me, "Your husband came in here and demanded that he had to have the prescription right away. He told me that if I didn't give it to him, he was gonna sock me! He bought a big box of Kotex and everything."

Bill must have been so demanding and his attitude so terrible that this new druggist just gave him the prescription. Bill then took it down to another drugstore, Dominion Drugs on Portage Avenue. I don't know how long he'd had it there. So, Douglas was going to Dominion Drugs way down on Portage Avenue at Bill's request, not thinking anything of it.

Over Heating

Our house, for several years, was heated by a coal furnace. I think it was in the spring one year that Bill had put the fire on in the morning. The days could get quite warm, so I didn't add to the fire during the day. When Bill came home that night, he became angry because I'd let the fire go out. He went down into that basement, and when he came back up, he said, "That fire won't go out in a hurry!" I went down and had a look, and it scared me. He had piled coal right up to the top of the furnace, and everything was red in there. I thought, "He'll burn the house down!" So, I phoned the fire department. I told them I was nervous about the fire in our basement furnace and was afraid it was going to overheat.

So, the firemen came out. Now Bill was there when they came. He didn't say much to them, and they didn't say much to him. The fire department and the police department shared the same building, and I think the firemen understood the situation because of the many times I'd had to call the police in the past. So, they just opened up the outside front door and stayed around until the furnace cooled down.

These things were scary because they began to be more frequent. Bill was taking the pills, which were altering his mood, and he was becoming erratic. I couldn't tell for sure whether things were going from bad to worse because he thought he was doing great and was putting everything in order—even if that meant making a massive fire in the furnace. It wasn't funny.

The Kobrinsky Boat and Veterans' Affairs

At some point between 1957 and 1959, while Bill had had his shop behind the house, he had begun to do some work for a Dr. Kobrinsky. The doctor also had a boat that needed work, and Bill would have to go out of town on different weekends to work on the boat where it was housed in a "wet shop."

Over time, Bill began to talk to the doctor, and the doctor noticed that something was not right. Bill would say, "I don't know why I lose my memory." He told the doctor he didn't understand why, when he was spraying, the spray-gun would fall out of his hand. I didn't know about a lot of these difficulties Bill was having when he was working, but he talked to the doctor about everything.

It was a couple of years later that Dr. Kobrinsky learned that Bill was not a pensioned veteran and began the process of helping him to apply for a pension. The doctor was able to get Bill's file from the Department of Veterans' Affairs. In the application for pension, Kobrinsky contended that the medical officers in the army had not gone far enough in investigating Bill's condition. They only tested for sleeping sickness and equine encephalitis, both of which came up negative. On the medical chart overseas, they put "Nil" for the test results, indicating that he didn't have either disease. When Bill had recovered to a certain point, he was assigned to work in the office in Trafalgar Square instead of being sent to the front lines. Bill was tested again for the same things before being discharged, and again the results were negative. Therefore, Bill had been deemed not pensionable.

The application for pension that Dr. Kobrinsky submitted was denied, but he told Bill and me that this was normal procedure—that's what the army would do—and now we would appeal that decision.

Bill had been confiding in Dr. Kobrinsky about everything, including all the trouble he'd had with the Hudson's Bay Company. He told him everything. The doctor told Bill he would need to put Bill in the hospital, saying, "I think I know what your problem is, but I have to have tests done to prove it, and they're not the easiest."

One test was an ECG (electrocardiogram) done in the Health Sciences Centre, and another test was done at the Saint Boniface Hospital. As I understand it, they put air into the spinal column at the bottom of the spine, and it would travel up into the head and illuminate what was happening there. He was supposed to lie flat on his back after that for a particular length of time, but he got up and tried to find a urinal. He didn't know what he was doing. They should have had somebody there to watch him. However, they injected a dye solution, which showed the circulation of blood in the head. There was no in-filling in the left carotid artery. This meant that blood wasn't getting up into the head. This apparently had been the problem when Bill had had the spell overseas.

Dr. Kobrinsky called when the test results were in, and Bill and I went in to get the findings. The doctor informed us that what Bill had had overseas was a cerebral haemorrhage, a leakage in the brain. He told us that about ninety percent of people with brain haemorrhages died and only about ten percent survived. Bill had survived. It was now fourteen years since Bill had returned from overseas.[31]

Around this time, I made arrangements to start a Licensed Practical Nursing course. Bill couldn't continue to cope with the pressure of running his shop. When Bill would have spells and spend time in the hospital, then, of course, there would be no income. Dr. Kobrinsky said it was good for Bill to have furniture finishing as a hobby, but he could see that Bill couldn't make a living at it.

Events after the Pension Hearing

Bill had a .22 revolver that his dad had given him. I knew it was still around, and he kept the bullets on the top shelf of a cupboard. One night, Bill was upstairs, and it appeared that Bill intended to use the gun, but Dan intercepted him. What Bill had had in mind I didn't know. I was getting more nervous and frightened.

The next day, I asked Bill about it: "Do you remember last night?"

He said, "No, I only know I was mad, I was mad." He couldn't remember what he had done.

I don't know if Bill ever told Dr. Kobrinsky about this, but I think those things frightened him, too. They were happening so often. I think that's why Bill would drink, too. He was trying to relieve the tension in his head.

To bring in some money, I had been doing babysitting and was also doing housework for Mrs. Shackell's mother from four to seven in the evenings. While I was there one time, Bill phoned me and said, "I just want you to know that everything is okay here." He had never done that before. The

---

[31] Dr. Kobrinsky also contended that Bill should not have gone to jail, that his medical and mental health condition should have exonerated him, as he was not in his right mind and could not exercise good judgement. See Dr. Kobrinsky's Discovery: January 12, 1960, letter to S. Kobrinsky from G. Fischer, M.D.

fact that he had phoned me to say that everything was alright made me realize that it wasn't alright. I phoned home, and Dan answered. I asked, "Is there anything wrong with Dad?" His reply was, "Well, he's walking around here with a wet towel on his head." I asked Dan to come and get me, and I told Mrs. Shackell that I had to go home.

When I got there, Bill had a wet towel around his head, and I learned he had taken a pill. I phoned the doctor and told him what was going on. He wanted to know where the pain was, so I asked Bill if he could tell the doctor. He said that he could, and he told the doctor that it was from the front of his head and over the top all the way to the back. The doctor told me to take Bill to Deer Lodge Hospital.

It was evening when I got Bill there, and I had to go to the admitting office. A man sitting at the desk asked me why Bill was there. I didn't like to say too much in front of Bill, but I felt I had to. I said, "It's because he's gotten so violent. I can't live with the violence. Doctor Kobrinsky told me to bring him here and get him admitted."

So, Bill was admitted. When I went to see him later, he was in a room with a lot of soldiers off to one end of the hospital. Bill said to me, "It's just like Christmas around here with these nuts. Get me out of here." That was kind of funny. But that's the way Bill was. It was a good thing he still had some humour left. I told him I'd see what I could do.

When I went to see Bill the next time, he was on another floor, the second floor, I think. He suggested we go down to the canteen. He had a dressing gown on. We walked down the hallway to get on the elevator to go down to the canteen. I noticed that when he was walking, he would veer off to one side. He couldn't walk straight.

The Hole in the Wall

When Bill was working at the shop, I had to go down to the welfare department at the end of each month and tell them what he had made. That would determine if we got welfare or not. One time, he had done pretty well, so they took us off welfare for that month. Bill didn't know whether to be mad at me or mad at them or mad at someone else, but it threw him for a loop. He was terrified that he wouldn't have the backing of welfare. He became furious. I just backed up and backed up. He was so angry that he punched his fist right into the wall.

Phillip was just a little boy then. Dan had just come in. He quickly took Phillip out the back door, went around to the front and then went two doors down to where an older couple we knew lived. In the meantime, I went out the front door. I went over to the Chornenkis' place (another family we knew) on Brooklyn Street and phoned the police. At the time, I didn't know that Dan had taken Phillip and stayed out of sight.

There was a big Carl's Meats[32] van behind the shop across the back alley from our house. After my phone call, I hid behind the van and watched to see what would happen when the police came. I saw Bill leave through the side door of the house and go over to Brooklyn Street. A little bit after he got away, the police car came.

I said to the police, "I'm not sure where he is, but he walked over toward Brooklyn Street."

So, they walked over, and I walked over, too.

There was a little boy there who asked, "Are you looking for a man?"

I said, "Yes."

Pointing, he said, "He went in that house."

I don't know what prompted that little boy to say that. But then I remembered that there *was* a fellow down that street that Bill knew. Bill had gone into his house.

I learned sometime later from Bill what happened. He was down in the basement of this man's house, and they both had shirts that were the same colour. The other man was a little bit bigger. The police went into the house, and the man's wife was there. They told her that they wanted to

---

[32] Carl's Meats was located across the back lane behind the Berry Street house. The business was short-lived.

talk to Frank Hay (Bill's legal name). She said he was downstairs with her husband, so one of them went down.

The policeman saw the two men and asked, "Okay, which of you is Frank Hay?"

Bill said, "He is."

Now, that was Bill. Afterward, Bill told me the policeman put his hands on the other guy, who said, "I am not. He is."

Then Bill said, "I know what you're here for. It's alright. I'll come."

So, Bill went with them, and they took him to Deer Lodge Hospital. He was there for a while.

When Frank came home from school, he came through the front door, and in the hall he found a hole in the wall.

Pension Review Result and the LPN Course

The pension review was on November 15, 1961, and I started my course on January 8, 1962. It was a one-year course.

In February, we heard that Bill would be pensioned and we would soon know the terms of the pension. Dr. Kobrinsky's effort on our behalf had been successful, and now we were "anchored."

In the end, it was seventy percent of a full pension that they granted us. I felt it should have been a hundred percent. In May 1962, the first bunch of money came by cheque and was for Bill. The Veterans' Affairs Department would pay for his hospitalization, and all his medication would be covered from that time on. The pension was retroactive. Another cheque came in June 1962 and was for me and the children. It was quite a large lump sum, around three or four thousand dollars. I put it in the bank. I don't remember what Bill did with his money. I think he was feeling relieved that he could do what he wanted to some extent.

Even though the pension money arrived, I didn't quit the nursing course. I didn't think that would be a very good thing to do. At one point while I was taking the course, Bill ended up in hospital for a while. I had been out at Ninette, Manitoba, doing a practicum.[33]

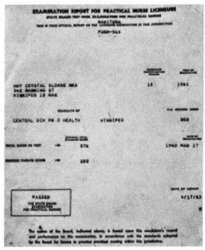

Crystal's graduation and LPN exam results

Phillip would be turning six in September 1962. Faith had turned nine in February. Both Phillip and Faith would be in Britannia School down the street. Frank, turning thirteen in August, was there, too, in grade seven. Doug was now in high school at St. James Collegiate.

The Banning Street House

The city of Winnipeg decided it was going to close down Madison Street to put in a subway through to St. James Street, by Polo Park. A Mr. Johnson, who had a painting business in that area, now had to find a new place for his business. I was still doing my LPN courses when Mr. Johnson came to talk to Bill to see if he would be interested in selling our property. That Berry Street location had been good while we had it, and it was going up in value. It was

---

[33] Sometime during the time that she was in Ninette, Dan had to take Faith to the hospital for an emergency appendectomy. Also, on the August long weekend, Dan got married. Mom had those four August days off.

130

now an expensive corner lot, and it would be a good investment, especially since the city was planning to widen Ness Avenue. A deal was made in about October that year, to sell. That was good for us.

We found a house at 543 Banning Street that would suit us, and we were told we could move into it in January 1963.

When life is happening, you can't see the whole picture. But, when I look back, I think that Bill wanted the house on Banning more than anything. I think it reminded him of his home on Toronto Street, and, as well, he would be closer to his sisters.

Poor Bill. He was so very sad, having suffered blow after blow. We lost the little girl. His mother died when he was overseas. Gertie swindled him out of everything. His dad had died at the Hudson's Bay store. He wanted Gertie to come and have Christmas dinner with us, and she wouldn't. He told me one time that he dropped in to where Gertie was working. She was at her counter, looking into a cupboard or something. When she looked up and saw him, she made sure he knew that she was not pleased to see him at all. When he was in Deer Lodge Hospital those many times, his family never came to see him. When he was out at Headingley Jail, they never came to see him. When he came home from overseas, they never came down to the train to meet him. What was he to do with things like that? It seemed that nobody cared about him. And it was even more difficult because I wasn't always the kindest, sweetest thing on earth. I tried to be, but I was in the middle of all of this, too.

All of these things affected Bill. When I look back, the move to Banning Street was not a good thing for us. It would have been good for Bill to still have had his shop. I think that's one more thing that disturbed him after we moved. He had no shop, and he couldn't seem to make any friends. It was the dead of winter, and we had only been there for three weeks before Bill took his own life.

PART THREE

CONCLUSION

EPILOGUE

Early on the morning of February 7, my father was found dead by hanging. I am told his last thoughtful act the night before he died was to repair the washing machine located in the basement.

We children were not in school that day. The teachers were at a conference and, classes were not in session. Dan was called, and the police, dressed in heavy winter coats and fur hats, picked him up at work to take him to the house. They told him what had transpired.

Dad left behind his wife of twenty-three years and four children still at home, aged five to fifteen, and one twenty-one-year-old married son.

Some of the reasons suggested for why our dad removed himself from us can be listed easily:

1. The house was now mortgage free.

2. The pension was in place to help his family.

3. Mom could now work and make a living as a Licensed Practical Nurse.

4. He would be released from his own suffering, for which no cure had been found.

Only God knew his heart and mind.

Thus far in this book, not much has been said about my father's religious and spiritual experiences. Mom talked about these on only a few occasions. But I feel it would be a disservice to the family, whom Mom raised within the context of a Christian community from the 1940s to the 1960s, not to mention it here. Most of Mom's family have at least some fond memories of church meetings and events we participated in, and some of us continue to be involved in church.

Mom did say that she and Dad would go to some church meetings together, and sometimes they had good discussions afterward. At one particular meeting, Dad became emotional and spoke with those who were there. The pastor prayed with him, and he was baptized the following week.

Matters of one's heart and faith should be told by the person himself. I cannot presume to know how our dad navigated those waters.

There was much of which Mom was unaware. This may be a gentle way of saying that she had knowingly or unknowingly been deceived. She never read her husband's first confession that he wrote out at the Hudson's Bay Company. She was not present at the speedy trial, at which his second written confession was given as evidence. The testimonies of the witnesses and the confession were very revealing.

In later years, Mom and Gertie seemed to have reconciled. We were really the only family Aunt Gertie had left. Cora passed away in 1968. Gertie remained in that same house on Toronto Street until she was hospitalized in the late summer of 1984, at age seventy-three. I was at her bedside when she breathed her last breath. Her house had always had a feeling of dark mystery about it, and I still felt it when I entered it as the executor of her estate after she was gone. When Gertie died and was buried with her parents and sister, no headstone was installed.

There seemed to be a general feeling among her descendants, and possibly their friends and relatives, that a memorial was not warranted. This was possibly due to leftover feelings of betrayal. However, once again, I felt that this needed to be rectified, that I should "finish the job" of reconciliation that my mother had started, that grace and forgiveness required a visual statement. I contacted the cemetery and a stonemasonry company to have a memorial marker installed. My brothers approved. Our feeling was that part of the story would now have a conclusion, a rightful end.

Between January 1962 and April 1963, while taking her nursing course, Mom had four children still at home, and Dad was in and out of hospital. Before her course ended, the pension approval came through in February. Doug turned fifteen in April. The pension money began to flow in May and June. Mom's own mother died in July 1962. Frank turned thirteen in August. Phil had his sixth birthday in September. Mom packed and then unpacked all of the family's household goods in the dead of winter, during the Christmas season, when we moved from Berry Street to Banning Street in January 1963. Three weeks after the move, her husband died on a cold February day, and the funeral took place two days later. I doubt that she and I celebrated our birthdays that month. Six weeks after Bill was gone, on March 27, she wrote her LPN exam. Her dad died a week later, on April 3. She received her marks from her LPN exam on April 17—she had passed with flying colours. Mom's determination and strength during that period borders on the miraculous.

Mom continued to live on Banning Street for ten to twelve more years. Doug, whose late teenage years were fraught with what seemed like "teenage rebellion," moved out a year or two after Dad's death. Frank, at age nineteen, moved to an apartment with two other guys, staying there until he eventually married. I, too, married and moved out in 1973. A year or so later, Mom sold the house. By that time,

Phil, the last of her children, had also moved out. I used to wonder why she stayed so long in the same house in which her husband had committed suicide.

The four children who moved to Banning Street with Dad and Mom were not told what had actually happened that February day. It was only years later that we were told, one by one, as adults, after we had left home. Prior to that, we had been led to believe that Dad had died of a brain haemorrhage. In a way, I guess it was true. It had just taken an awfully long time.

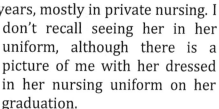

Mom's Later Years

Mom would have been close to sixty years old when she left the Banning Street house. We know that she used her nursing skills over the years, mostly in private nursing. I

don't recall seeing her in her uniform, although there is a picture of me with her dressed in her nursing uniform on her graduation.

After selling the house, Mom never settled for long in any one place—until she bought her apartment and moved into Lindenholm Place, built by the church, in 1989. She remained happily there until her death in the spring of 2004, at age eighty-eight. Prior to that, Mom had "followed" my husband and me as we also moved from place to place in our early married years, in order to be close to us.

As grandchildren came along, Mom loved and cherished all of them and supported the expanding families as best she could. Her church community continued to be an important aspect of her life. She took joy in music, both singing in the church choir and playing piano at home. She continued to have supportive friendships and developed more, and she was able to enjoy a few holiday ventures. Of significance was a trip with her friend

The holiday trip with Mom, Phil, Faith. Louisa Steves and her little dog

Louisa Steves, a widow who had a little dog, a car and a trailer. Not long after Dad passed away, Louisa invited Mom,

Mom made this painting in a painting class at Lindenholm Place in 1992-1993.

Phil and me to join her on a trip from Winnipeg to Tijuana, Mexico, back up the west coast and then east to Winnipeg. Phil and I have mixed reviews of that holiday.

In later years, Mom visited her granddaughter and family in Germany. She went on a bus tour to Glorietta, New Mexico, and she took a trip on her own to help out a missionary family in Panama for several weeks.

In her senior years, Mom participated in an advertisement for We Care, a service that provided care for seniors in their own homes, of which she had been a client.

Mom also helped to make history at the Brookside Cemetery by arranging for the disinterment of her first, stillborn child, as well as her husband Bill from the military section. They were then re-interred together in a new plot in the civilian section. Bill's headstone had room for Mom's name and dates, which she arranged to have partially engraved. The engraving was completed after her own death in March 2004, when she was buried with them. Our understanding is that this was the first time the cemetery had performed such a task.

As Sparks Fly Upward

The title of this book is taken from Job 5:6-7 (NIV):

"For hardship does not spring from the soil,
nor does trouble sprout from the ground.
Yet man is born to trouble
as surely as sparks fly upward."

These verses from Scripture explain that hardship and trouble, like brambles and thistles, do not just rise up from the dust of the earth by chance, but are natural to the cursed earth. In our fallen state, it has become natural for us to sin.

Following the impulses of our evil nature, we can bring affliction on ourselves.

Sin is thus the root and cause of all the sorrow and suffering of humankind. But that does not mean that a particular individual is suffering because of personal sin. Jesus Christ, our Saviour, did no wrong, committed no sin whatever, yet he suffered the agony of the cross. Christ's disciples asked Jesus the question about a man born blind, "Who sinned, this man or his parents, that he was born blind?" (John 9:2). Jesus put that old lie to rest with the declaration that neither the blind man nor his parents had sinned, but that he was born blind so that the work of God might be displayed in his life. Then, Jesus restored the man's vision. Mom might have been born to trouble, but the work of God could also be seen in Mom's life.

Our family certainly had its beginnings in troubled times and had its share of trouble. How was our mother able to carry on through it all? Mom had the following poem taped to the inside of her kitchen cupboard wherever she lived, beginning in the Berry Street house:

> *God has not promised skies always blue,*
> *flower-strewn pathways all our lives through;*
> *God has not promised sun without rain,*
> *joy without sorrow, peace without pain.*
> *But God has promised strength for the day,*
> *rest for the labor, light for the way,*
> *grace for the trials, help from above,*
> *unfailing sympathy, undying love.*[34]
>
> *– Faith Fisher*

---

[34] Annie Johnson Flint, "God Hath Not Promised."

Brief Reflections of the Children

Dan witnessed the events of our family life over a longer period of time. Re-visiting the story brought back painful memories and stirred deep emotion in him. While choking back tears, he managed to convey the memory of standing by a window, looking out, waiting and wondering if his dad would come home on Christmas Eve.

He still feels anger towards those at the Hudson's Bay Company whom he believes trapped Dad and used him.

Dan does, however, have keen memories of happy times—visits to Grandpa and Grandma's farm, playing on the haystacks, and consuming handfuls of honeycomb—honey, wax, bees and all—from a neighbour's barrel stored at the farm. He also has memories of building snow forts, of fires and of the go-cart he constructed out of scrap crates and baby carriage parts.

Over the years, Dan reconciled, within himself and before God, the events of the past. He moved on with life, understanding how the past was a determiner of his later behaviours and perspectives. He tucked the past away. He became stoic. He had learned to pray during those hard times and developed a deep faith.

With **Doug**'s passing in 2019, his reflections on this story are, regretfully, missing. I am sure he would have had much to contribute. However, everyone knew of Doug's love of music, and I personally believe that is what "centred" him and throughout his life gave it meaning.

Frank became a history buff. There is very little he couldn't tell about the life of Winston Churchill. In some way, out of his admiration for Mr. Churchill, Frank "adopted" him as a father figure.

Phil, the youngest of the family, reminded me that, with Dad's death, Mom became a single parent. It placed a designation on her, and, by extension, on our life from that point on, that I had not previously considered. Phil was just six years old when Dad died, and he has limited memory of his early childhood.

– Faith Fisher

Frank, Faith, Dan, Doug, Phil, first sibling fishing trip, 2004

Appendix 1
The First Confession

May 28, 1952
Statement Filed as Exhibit Three
I, Frank Wm Hay

Do humbly confirm to participating in or with acknowledgement of the disposing of goods, the property of the Hudson's Bay Department Store. I do this with unburdened heart and will give the truth and nothing but the truth.

Roughly two years ago, I was approached by individuals working within the store to sell them small radios for their disposal. At first, I did not do so but, gradually after taking the first few dollars, the circle grew bigger. These individuals are not now with the Company. In name, they were Alex Faires, Syd Donovan, Clarence Nash, and Clarence Morris. These so-called transactions were not easy as I knew the differences of right and wrong. For months on end, I used to try to avoid doing anything of detriment to my department and for even several years made no effort to comply with others' wishes.

After the war, when I came back and was again received into The Company, my desire was to do the right thing, but gradually the encroachments of living, raising a family, the opportunity to make a few easy, dishonest dollars rose again. I fell to the lure but not in any large way. I knew, however, of others; one John Summack, who was employed in the Service Department as an outside washing machine mechanic, who was getting away with hundreds of dollars, not only from the Service Department but, from my own Department stock also. He was caught through my efforts and discharged. I did nothing wrong in regards to stealing anything myself, however many opportunities I had.

I was given the opportunity of being in charge of the Piano Shop, which entails refinishing and repairing pianos. I was happy to carry on with this work that I knew and loved to do until last June when, after returning from holidays found the shop I had worked so hard at and making a good job in destroyed and tools and equipment spread from one end of the sixth floor to the other. Inexcusable as it may be, I was filled with bitterness and almost a vengeance and started to drink heavily.

To carry on, I needed a little extra money. Alex Faires and Cliff Reid were available and either with my knowledge or assistance disposed of about 10 small radios. About this time, I discovered that one Alex Mills was stealing and disposing of sets from the sixth floor.

More to cover myself than from loyalty to The Company, I put myself in the position of informing Mr. Kennedy, and in due time, Alex Mills, Nels Courage, Clarence Morris, Alex Faires were involved, along with Freddie..., who was then working at The Victor Company. Mr. Dargie knows of the details of their apprehension and discharge.

Somehow the worry and strain, the entanglements, made me see that I was even worse than even they were, and, instead of straightening up and owning up, I went from bad to worse. I continued to drink and needed money, and when Jim Duane[35] or Boivin came, I approached him in regards to making a deal. He was as eager as I was to have some extra money, and when Funk of New Bothwell came in and seemed interested in getting a washer for 60 dollars, the deal went as planned. Jim got a C.O.G.[36] bill signed and

---

[35] James Duane started working at the Hudson's Bay Company in March 1952. After he had been there for three days, Bill took him out for a beer, bragging to Duane that he had been working for the company for seventeen years and had never been caught for theft. James, although serving time in Headingley Jail, was brought out to appear in court and was identified at Bill's trial.

[36] Customer Owned Goods.

the washer put on the shipping platform. The arrangement was that Funk would have a truck pick it up. He paid us 30 dollars the day the deal was made, and I think it was a Tuesday that he made the trip in and paid the balance of $15.00. This deal was split 30 dollars apiece.

After this, Jim and I became friendly through drinking and planned a couple of more washer deals. Through the drinking, I guess I wanted to show him I knew all the angles and talked big. He has a brother or father in the washing machine repair business, but, after meeting him, I will not go ahead on anything further.

I must mention the motor, used value of about 5 dollars, that I carried out to Funk's car. I received $3.00 for it and in turn split it with Jim. When Funk came in again one time about 3 weeks ago, Jim sold him 3 used motors. I didn't take anything of a split. Surprising enough though it may be, I do not believe anyone in the Service Department Office knew what was going on in regards to the bills for the motors or the washer, and until more rigid check is made on bills in the Service Department, it would be easy to send out merchandise the same way as the washer.

I estimate that the most I received in cash would be about $600 dollars, just what the retail would be I can only double the above figure.

I sold two other items, 1 washer and 1 combination radio to H. Cook, 614 Cambridge.

Appendix 2
The Second Confession

Given to and written by Elmer Thorne, Winnipeg Police, in the presence of Detective Benzie
Signed by Bill, Thorne and Benzie
From Court Documents
May 28, 1952, 6:15 p.m.
Statement Filed as Exhibit Four
As given by Frank William Hay, 37 years of age, married and residing at 313 Berry Street, St. James:

"I have been employed with the Hudson Bay Company for the past 15 years. During this time, I have worked in the Radio and Appliance Department, also in the Piano Finishing Shop. During my employ in this Department, I have known of several of the other employees stealing radios, etc. These men have either quit or have been fired. Since being employed with them I have taken, to my knowledge, approximately 12 or 15 small radios throughout the past 15 years. During the past 3 months, I have taken out of the store or had it picked up 1 radio combination, believe it is a Baycrest, 1 washing machine. Both of these articles I sold to Harold Cook of 614 Cambridge Street for the sum of $125.00. I also sold a Thor washer to a man by the name of Funk living in New Bothwell, Manitoba. I also sold him 1 washing machine motor for $3.00. I got $60.00 for the washing machine. Funk knew I was stealing the stuff as he asked me how I was going to get it out of the store. I had no access to any of the bills for the goods, and I needed an accomplice, who is Jim Duane. He has only been with the Company a short time. He was able to get a bill known as a C.O.G. (Customers Own Goods) which had to be signed for by a person with a signature in The Bay. The goods could then be delivered. The radio and washer I sold to Cook and got $125.00 for. Cliff Reid who was at that time working for The Bay, got $25.00 or $30.00 of this money. He was the Assistant Shipper at The Bay. I had always talked fairly fluently when drinking and had mentioned to individuals that I had taken out articles such as a piano and fridges but which I never did steal. Sometime in around about 1947, I sold a small mantle radio to Clarence Morris, who was working at the store at that time. I got $5.00 for it."

Appendix 3
Other Testimony
from the Court Documents

Elmer Thorne: "As a result of conversation with the accused's wife, I interviewed the accused later, and he told me he had two articles at his own home, 313 Berry Street, St. James, which he had bought—received from ex-employees of the Hudson's Bay Company—which he was paid very little money for. On the 29th of May at 3:45 p.m., we attended at the accused's home, 313 Berry Street, St. James, where the wife of the accused handed over to us a Royal Floor Polisher serial number 651087 and Goblin Vacuum Cleaner Serial 55C-71195. These two articles are here on the floor." (Bill was not charged for the theft of these.)

James Duane: [Bill was] "a shipper at the Hudson's Bay. I was working in the washing machine shop...About 3 days of the week after I was in there, he [Bill] asked me to go out for a beer with him. We went to the Army and Navy. He told me he was the person who could make a little bit of money on the side and that he had been working for seventeen years and had never been caught at it—that all we had to do was get C.O.G.s...One night, he [Bill] told me he had a book [of C.O.G.s] worth $5,000.00 that he got for $5.00—you could buy them in the Bay."

Appendix 4
Dr. Kobrinsky's Discovery

Dad carried the letter from Dr. Kobrinsky in his wallet until he died. The last paragraph in the summary indicates that the process resulting in his present condition "had been going on for many years" and it was "quite possible" that the "process was already going on while he was in Service."

Therefore, it is quite likely that the condition began in June 1942, when Bill was treated for symptoms that Dr. McGrier had assumed were indicative of neuralgia. The symptoms of a brain haemorrhage may include sudden or severe headache, weakness, tingling or numbness in arms or legs, nausea/vomiting, changes in vision and/or balance, difficulty in speaking or understanding speech, seizures and loss of consciousness (catatonia). In her story, Mom describes Dad as experiencing many of these symptoms.

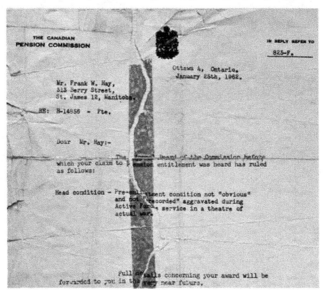

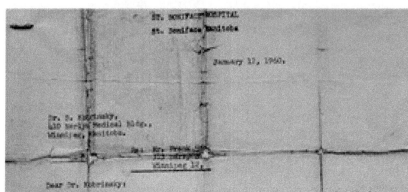

ST. BONIFACE HOSPITAL

St. Boniface, Manitoba

January 12, 1960.

Dr. S. Skorinsky,
410 Boyine Medical Bldg.,
Winnipeg, Manitoba.

Re: Mr. Frank ...
133 ....
Winnipeg 12.

Dear Dr. Skorinsky:

Thank you very much for referring the above-mentioned patient. As you state in your consultation request, the patient gives a prolonged history since 1942 when he developed headaches, slurred speech and a feeling of weakness and partial amnesia. This occurred while on leave. Because of this episode he was treated by his Unit for equine encephalitis. Skull X-rays taken at your office were reported to be normal and the lumbar puncture done at Deer Lodge Hospital was also found to be essentially normal. In 1955 showed low amplitude recording. Virus studies give no evidence of previous equine encephalitis. He now complains of intermittent episodes of stiffness in his right arm, with peculiar sensation at the back of the neck, which have become more pronounced during the past eight months. The patient is quite vague in explaining his difficulties and it is difficult to obtain an adequate history. A neurological examination on December 29 was essentially negative and since we suspected an atrophic cerebral lesion, a pneumo-encephalogram was suggested. This was carried out on December 30 and the report of Dr. C. W. Hall read as follows: "Good filling of the ventricular system has been obtained, no significant displacement or distortion of the lateral third ventricle. The fourth ...... basal cisterns appear normal. There ... some thickening of the .... of both cerebral hemispheres, somewhat ... marked on the left side ... the findings are consistent with a degree of cortical atrophy." The cerebrospinal fluid examination was again negative.

Because of the apparently sudden onset of symptoms we felt that we should rule out an intracranial vascular lesion and proceeded therefore with a bilateral carotid angiogram. Again, the report by Dr. C. W. Hall reads: "Left cerebral angiogram: Good filling of the internal carotid artery has been outlined and there is no filling of the anterior cerebral artery on the left side. The middle cerebral vessels are normal in distribution. They are however of rather small calibre. Air remains in the lateral ventricle from previous pneumo-encephalogram.

154

There is also some air over the frontal poles bilaterally."

"Right cerebral angiogram: Good filling of the internal carotid artery and its intracranial branches has been obtained. Cross filling occurs into the left anterior cerebral artery and there is no evidence of displacement or distortion of the anterior or middle cerebral vessels."

Other examinations done during the hospital stay are: Urinalysis- hematocrit 45%; 5.0 Red Blood cells, Color Index 1.00. Total white cells 7,700 and the differential: Neutrophils 48, Bands 14, Eosinophils 1, Lymphocytes 30 and Monocytes 7.

In summary, the investigation showed that this patient had cortical - brain atrophy which is not progressed so the relative narrow intracranial vessels. I am quite sure that this process has been going on for many years and according to the EEG not seem to be active at the present time. It is quite possible process was already going on while he was in the Service.

Sincerely yours,

G. Fischer, M.D.

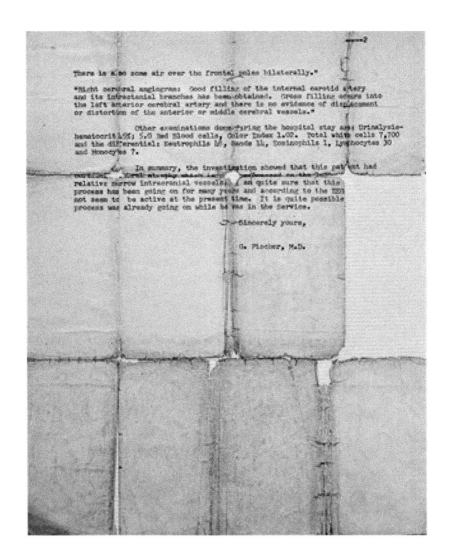

Appendix 5
Mom's Obituary

Crystal Hay, 88, went to be with her Lord and Saviour on March 21, 2004. A mother of two daughters and four sons, she had 17 grandchildren and 23 great-grandchildren. Crystal's first daughter predeceased her at birth, and husband, Frances William, in 1963. Crystal had a very strong faith which gave her strength, comfort and the resolve to overcome adversity. She helped others in ways that provided encouragement to all around her, including her family. As an active member of Grant Memorial Baptist Church, she was involved in many ways, including singing with the Golden Echoes. She travelled to Panama to assist in mission support work for the underprivileged. Crystal was a true people-person who loved to help others and, at mid-life, became a licensed practical nurse. She gave freely of herself as a youth camp nurse and cook. Her grandchildren and great-grandchildren received her unconditional love and life-long memories. Her acts of faith and love towards family, friends and those in her community was evident to all. For those who wish to mourn and say goodbye to Crystal, a viewing will be held at Neil Bardal Inc. at 984 Portage Ave., Aubrey Street entrance, on Thursday, March 25 between 2:00 p.m. and 4:00 p.m. Crystal's family wishes also to extend an invitation to those who knew her and wish to remember and celebrate her life, to join them at Grant Memorial Baptist Church, 877 Wilkes Ave. on Saturday, March 27 at 10:00 a.m.

– As published in Winnipeg Free Press on March 24, 2004

Appendix 6
Timeline

1936: Joseph and Mabel Sloane are living at 202 Harcourt Street, Winnipeg.

1939: Mom marries Bill Hay in October but continues to live with her parents at 202 Harcourt Street; Bill's parents find them a suite on Home Street; they buy furniture; Mom becomes pregnant.

1940: The family move back to Harcourt Street; Mom gives birth in November, but the baby is stillborn.

1941: The family move to Ingersoll Street; Dan is born in December.

1942: In June, Mom reports that Bill has neuralgia and is on sick leave from work.

1943: The family move back to 202 Harcourt Street.

1944: On October 30, Mom hosts a farewell party for Bill; Bill goes to the Fort Osborne barracks for two weeks and is then sent to Ontario.

1945: Bill becomes ill in Scotland while on leave; he is sent to London for the duration of his service; in the summer, Mom buys the house at 229 Parkhill Street; Bill's mother dies; Joseph and Mabel move to 3067 Portage Avenue along Sturgeon Creek.

1946: Bill returns from war duty in April; the family move to 279 Queen Street in November.

1947: Doug is born in April.

1949: The family move to 313 Berry Street; Frank is born.

1950: Bill's dad dies in late fall; the legal battle with Gertie begins; Bill starts working on the sixth floor of the Hudson's Bay Company repairing pianos.

1951: Bill has a spell of amnesia at home in March; the Hudson's Bay Company moves him back to the fourth floor;

Bill is angry and drinking too much; the thievery continues and becomes more serious.

1952: Bill is arrested, confesses and is sentenced.

1953: Faith is born in February; Bill is released to a halfway house in the summer.

1954: Bill sets up his shop behind Gibson's Bakery on Berry Street.

1955: Bill moves his business to Madison Street; his condition goes from bad to worse; about this time, Joseph and Mabel move to 519 Sprague Street; Doug spends time in the summer at Marie's place in Biggar, Saskatchewan.

1956: Phil is born in September.

1957-1959: Bill is in and out of Deer Lodge Hospital; his shop is now behind the house on Berry Street; he works on Dr. Kobrinsky's boat, and Dr. Kobrinsky takes on his case.

1960: The results from the tests done at St. Boniface Hospital arrive January 12; after a successful appeal, Bill is granted a veteran's pension.

1962: Mom starts the LPN course in January; her mother dies July 17; Mom does her practicum in Ninette; Dan marries August 4.

1963: The family move to Banning Street around January 17; Bill dies February 7; Mom writes her LPN exam March 27 (the minimum passing score is 350, and her score is 576); Mom's dad dies April 3; first grandchild born December 3.

Acknowledgements

As I stated in the Introduction, "Research was done to corroborate time, date, names, places, events and more." This book would not have come to fruition had it not been for the invaluable guidance, input and encouragement from others. I did not know that in this journey of discovery, I would be helped by willing strangers, be renewing acquaintances and be building friendships enroute.

I would, in particular, like to thank the following, some of whom I hope to soon meet:

• Holly Ross of Abbotsford, B.C., who assisted in the transcription of the original recording. I have yet to meet Holly, who was recommended by a mutual friend with whom she worked.

• N.J. Lindquist, author, Markham, Ontario. I believe it was providential that I met N.J. She and her husband Les led a writer's workshop in 2016 at House of James, Abbotsford, B.C. Thank you for setting me on the right path, providing the first instructions that led to organizing the content of the transcription.

• Jane and Eugene Rempel, friends and encouragers in the writing process. Jane has written her own memoir, writes poetry and creates visual art. We met at the same workshop led by N.J. Lindquist.

• Loraine Houston, my dear elder cousin in Red Deer, Alberta. Loraine is her family's historian and over several years compiled two huge volumes of family history. Besides mailing information back and forth, I was able to spend a few hours with her, viewing the pictures, documents and wealth of historical information she had compiled. Our stories cross, and she was able to corroborate or refute claims made in the story draft.

• Julienne Rwagasore, Winnipeg, Manitoba. A good friend, she provided helpful advice based on her experience with media. She answered my questions during a lovely four-hour lunch.

• Marilyn Giesbrecht (nee Bystrom). Our friendship goes a long way back to our youth and our church affiliation. Thank you for meeting me at The Park Café after all these years and confirming a section of Mom's story.

• Diane Epp, Winnipeg, Manitoba, a friend and long-time member of Grant Memorial Baptist Church, who, despite the unfortunate disarray of the church's archived material, provided some helpful insights.

• Jane Shackell, Vancouver, B.C. I hope to yet meet you in person. I don't think I will ever forget how I came to connect with you. The first step was spelling the name correctly! Thank you for your willingness to look for and provide the picture of your grandparents, Claude and Mildred Shackell, as well as the picture of their grocery store. Claude and Mildred endeared themselves to our family and remain dear to us.

• Fred Morris, St. James historian, Winnipeg, Manitoba, who undertook research and provided helpful information about the location of 3067 Portage Avenue. He also provided information on the use of Winnipeg's Henderson Directories. That was an invaluable resource. Thank you!

• Ashley, Julianna and Vince at the Archives of Manitoba, who were patient, knowledgeable and interested on the several occasions I visited there, helping me to find the pertinent criminal case files and some Hudson's Bay Company material of the period in question.

• Stuart, Heidi and Rachel in the Library Archives of Manitoba, who introduced me to the Henderson Directories that I had no idea existed, as well as government and private sector archives. Thank you for helping me find articles from the *Winnipeg Free Press* and the *Winnipeg Tribune* newspapers, including obituaries and birth announcements. I learned that spelling was important!

• James R. Coggins, Mill Lake Books, Abbotsford, B.C. I'm glad I found you on the internet! Reaching out to you in the early stages of pre-publishing, I was a fish out of water. Thank you, Jim, for taking me on, for your insight, patience and encouragement along this seemingly long road.

• My other supportive friends and family. Thank you for walking with me. Too numerous to name, you know who you are. Thank you, my brothers, for your reflections, perspectives and support.

• Mom. Thank you for your example of what it means to push up through the difficult, heavy soil of life and bloom where you are planted.

– Faith Fisher

Printed in the USA
CPSIA information can be obtained
at www.ICGtesting.com
JSHW010706170424
61304JS00001B/2